BUSINESS ISSUES, COMPETITION AND ENTREPRENEURSHIP

TECHNOLOGY MANAGEMENT IN INTERNATIONAL ENTREPRENEURSHIP

INNOVATIVE DEVELOPMENT AND SUSTAINABILITY

Business Issues, Competition and Entrepreneurship

Additional books and e-books in this series can be found on Nova's website under the Series tab.

BUSINESS ISSUES, COMPETITION AND ENTREPRENEURSHIP

TECHNOLOGY MANAGEMENT IN INTERNATIONAL ENTREPRENEURSHIP

INNOVATIVE DEVELOPMENT AND SUSTAINABILITY

OLGA A. SHVETSOVA

nova science publishers
New York

NOTICE TO THE READER

The Publisher has taken reasonable care in the preparation of this book, but makes no expressed or implied warranty of any kind and assumes no responsibility for any errors or omissions. No liability is assumed for incidental or consequential damages in connection with or arising out of information contained in this book. The Publisher shall not be liable for any special, consequential, or exemplary damages resulting, in whole or in part, from the readers' use of, or reliance upon, this material. Any parts of this book based on government reports are so indicated and copyright is claimed for those parts to the extent applicable to compilations of such works.

Independent verification should be sought for any data, advice or recommendations contained in this book. In addition, no responsibility is assumed by the Publisher for any injury and/or damage to persons or property arising from any methods, products, instructions, ideas or otherwise contained in this publication.

This publication is designed to provide accurate and authoritative information with regard to the subject matter covered herein. It is sold with the clear understanding that the Publisher is not engaged in rendering legal or any other professional services. If legal or any other expert assistance is required, the services of a competent person should be sought. FROM A DECLARATION OF PARTICIPANTS JOINTLY ADOPTED BY A COMMITTEE OF THE AMERICAN BAR ASSOCIATION AND A COMMITTEE OF PUBLISHERS.

Additional color graphics may be available in the e-book version of this book.

Library of Congress Cataloging-in-Publication Data

Names: Shvetsova, Olga A., Korea University of Technology and Education, Byeongcheon-meyon, Cheonan City, Chungnam Province, South Korea, author.
Title: Technology Management in International Entrepreneurship: Innovative Development and Sustainability
Description: New York: Nova Science Publishers, [2019] | Series: Business Issues, Competition and Entrepreneurship | Includes bibliographical references and index.
Identifiers: LCCN 2019954656 (print) | ISBN 9781536167771 (paperback) |
ISBN 9781536167788 (adobe pdf)

Published by Nova Science Publishers, Inc. † New York

CONTENTS

ABSTRACT

This book is focused on theoretical bases of technology management in global environment. Author analyses different approaches of innovation creation and development. Main innovative strategies are discussed within different external and internal circumstances. This book is focused on theoretical and practical bases of technology management in global environment. Author analyses different approaches of technology transferring and development in global markets. Global environment analysis, global markets classification and innovations' transferring process are discussed. The main idea of this book is sustainable strategy development for global technology companies.

The first chapter refers to recent trends in global innovations' environment: global factors, markets, trends and risks are discussed. The second chapter refers to legal and theoretical aspecs of technology entrepreneurship. The third chapter refers to global trends of external and internal environments: environmental analysis, structure and concepts are discussed. The fourth chapter refers to the best practices of global companies in technology management: global leadership through innovations, transferring innovations and problems of customization are discussed. The fith chapter refers to different models of innovations: core competencies, 4th Industrial revolution and global partnership of global corporations are discussed. The last chapter discusses strategic approaches of global technology entreprenuership.The theoretical approaches are extracted and discussed with different authors cross over the world; practical material is based on the best practices of global corporations.

The material is prepared on the basis of market research of enterprises and organizations of various forms of ownership in different countries. The theoretical approaches are extracted and discussed with different authors cross over the world.

The publication is intended for specialists in the field of higher professional education institutions, as well as for a wide range of researchers, postgraduates and graduate students within any economic specialties.

Keywords: technology management; entrepreneurship; sustainability; global environment; innovative development

INTRODUCTION

For the development of innovation, a favorable infrastructure is necessary, where technologies could not only "emerge", but also receive further development. To date, large funds are allocated from the budget of any country to create and develop comfortable conditions that can stimulate production (Aarons G, et al., 2009, 1083-1097). It is possible to single out a whole series of "organized" territories in accordance with the type of innovation, such as: techno parks; science cities; closed administrative-territorial entities; technical and innovation zones; academic campus. The purpose of these organizations is the creation of new technologies and their introduction into production, and it is at the stage of direct commercialization of technology or in other words the transfer of technology (innovation) into the business sphere that complications arise in the economy.

It is important to note that the leaders of the world market, to date, become the owners of technology, moreover, not only those who managed to introduce a new technology once, but those who constantly produce new products or introduce new innovations, or improve already available technologies. The main tool that realizes the relationship between the developers of innovations (technologies) and its recipient can become a "technology transfer" (Backer T, et al., 1986, 111-123). This process will be described in detail and assessed from the point of view of the effectiveness of application in the structure of innovation activity.

Nowadays there is rapidly changing global economy, and technological innovation has become more important due to technology trajectory, short product life cycle, and globalization. It is necessary to develop new models of planning in project-management and transferring technologies to achieve sustainability in global markets. For automobile industry, acquiring innovative technologies can be a source of a firm's long term success. Technology strategy has become one of the most significant factors for a firm to consider when making a business decision. There are two ways to obtain technology to increase a firm's competitiveness: self-R&D and technology transfer.

Parker, D., et al. (1998, 98-103) suggested that technology transfer is a strategic component of innovation activity. According to the efficient implementation of the technologies' transmission mechanism industry can intensify the implementation and development processes of high-tech innovations in production activities and get additional competitive advantages. Effective technology transfer accelerates innovation processes at regional, national and transnational levels Aarons G, et al., 2011, 4-12). The study of the process of technological transfer is necessary to evaluate benefits of technology transfer and ways to achieve these benefits. Dyer (1998, 78) and Stuart (1988, 8) have studied the relationship characteristics between alliance partners, including the effects of the relative position and reputation of each partner firm, the strategic similarity of the firms, and their former relationship.

The commercialization of technology in developed and innovation-driven countries (USA, Germany, South Korea, etc.) is the foundation of global competitiveness, which actualizes the need for significant efforts to support and develop the production of knowledge, high technology and innovation in various fields of activity. One of the locomotives for the development of innovation is scientific activity, as a basis for the development of knowledge and the creation of high technology. Many empirical studies have examined how technology transfer influences investment of self-R&D expenditure. Most of authors (Odagiri et al., 1983;

Braga and Wilmore, 1991; Deolalikar and Evenson, 1993; Zhao, 1995; Hu et al., 2005) show that a complementary relationship does exist between technology transfer and self-R&D, confirming that there is a positive effect.

In global practice, the construction of the infrastructure for support innovation is carried out within a number of organizational forms, such as "Technopolice"; zones for the development of innovative and high technologies; science and technology parks; innovation and technology centers; and centers for the commercialization of technologies; business incubators (Simpson D., 2002, 15).

While innovation and growth are central for addressing social challenges, improving economic performance and creating jobs, the impacts are not necessarily "socially" inclusive, because they can increase inequalities in income and opportunities of different groups in society (Tabak R, et al., 2012, 390). A majority of the world's poor now live in middle-income countries where the inequalities in income and opportunities are strikingly skewed. The realities in many emerging and developing countries are such that a small fraction of the population has access to wider resources and opportunities while a larger group lacks access to the most basic resources. At the top of many government agendas is the objective of socially inclusive development, because high levels of inequalities can negatively affect growth.

Innovation dynamics and policies have impacts on "industrial inclusiveness", which is the extent to which firms differ in their innovation and productivity performance (Stetler C., 2001, 267). Many emerging and developing economies have economic structures characterized by "islands of excellence" - very innovative, world-leading businesses, sectors, research institutions or universities - which coexist with a group of weak performing firms or institutions and a substantial informal economy. Industrial inclusiveness has potentially important impacts on social inclusiveness. In addition, "territorial inclusiveness" - the geographic dimensions of industrial and social inequalities-is an important facet of those inequalities (Oldenburg B, et al., 2008, 315).

Thus, inclusive development is essential for innovation policy agendas in emerging countries, along with research aimed at addressing social challenges. Many examples show that innovative products, particularly in the areas of food, health and basic livelihood, can contribute substantially to improving the welfare of lower-income groups. Both private for-profit actors and not-for-profit actors have supported initiatives, with financial and other forms of aid. To serve lower-income markets, demand-side characteristics beyond high sensitivity to price, have to be addressed. Such demand-side characteristics are the need to adjust products to specific user contexts, such as lack of access to electricity, and the challenge of providing information about product purpose and use, reflecting the low human capital of most low-income groups. Entrepreneurs have used innovative pricing and financing strategies and business process innovations to serve lower-income markets profitably (OECD, 2013, 89).

Chapter 1

TECHNOLOGY MANAGEMENT IN GLOBAL ENVIRONMENT

1.1. CONCEPTS OF TECHNOLOGY MANAGEMENT, PRINCIPLES, METHODS, OBJECTIVES

The term "technology" (from the Greek "techne" - art, skill, skill) in the industrial sense is understood as a set of methods of processing, manufacturing, changing the state, properties, form of raw materials, material or semi-finished products that are produced in the production process (Perlitz M., 1997, 78).

In the broad sense of the interpretation of this concept, the term "technology" implies the production of material goods, which includes the following three components:

1. information - the process of describing the principles and methods of production;
2. social - the features of the organization of human capital in the production process;
3. instrumental - means of labor, through which production is realized.

Technology management implies a combination of methods of the control system's influence on the managed system, at which significant (visible) change of systems takes place, taking into account the use of modern scientific, technical, production, managerial and commercial knowledge and experience.

Technology, aimed at performing operations related to the processing of information, was called information. The orientation of information technology (IT) to the solution of tasks of entrepreneurship is considered as information technology in management.

Table 1. Comparative characteristics of technologies of material production and information technology

Technology of material production	Information technology
Changes the quality of material facilities with the aim of obtaining principally new products	Receiving primary data, they are processed using intelligence, in order to make an informed management decision
Applying different technologies to a single material resource, it is possible to obtain products of different kinds and grades, and of the same quality	Using different processes of processing one information, information of different quality is obtained
The means and methods of processing, manufacturing, changing the state, properties, form of raw materials or materials are used	Means and methods are used to mediate the collection, processing, accumulation, storage and transfer of data at an economic site
The goal is to produce products that meet the needs of a person or system	The goal is the collection and processing of information, on the basis of which well-founded management decisions are made

Source: Freemen Chr., Louca Fr. (2001) As time goes by: From the industrial revolution to the information// Oxford University Press, Oxford; N.Y., XV. p. 407.

Information technology in management is a process that uses a combination of methods and means to implement the collection, registration, transfer, accumulation and processing of information on the basis of software and hardware for the management of economic objects. The unity of the concepts “technology” and “information technology” lies in the fact that both are based on a process by which a certain set of actions aimed at achieving the stated goal is understood. Any technological process must be determined by a person's chosen strategy and implemented with the help of a combination of different methods and means.

Comparison of technology of material production and information technology is given in Table 1.

The principal difference between IT and technology of material production is that, in the first case, the technology cannot be continuous, in fact, combining the technology of routine work (production processes) and creative, often intuitive work (based on the abilities of critical analysis of data obtained during operational accounting).

The main features of management technologies include:

1. Management methods: in information technologies - methods of processing and transferring information; in social technologies - methods of group and individual action (and interaction); in instrumental technologies - management of innovations, modernization of production processes.
2. The purpose of management: the information technology process has to obtain information; social process has to develop the formation of a given behavior; instrumental has to use the equipment and equipment corresponding to the production process;
3. The subject of management: in information technology - the subject of processing are data; in social - perception of the surrounding reality; in instrumental - ways of choosing, using, storing and servicing the means of labor;
4. The means that carry out the technological process: in information technology - a variety of computer systems (software, hardware, communication); in social - infection, suggestion, imitation; in instrumental - the implementation of R&D;
5. Data processing is divided into operations in accordance with the chosen subject area of activity and the objectives of the enterprise management;

6. Management impacts on processes are carried out by the subjects of management that are part of the management structure of enterprises and organizations;
7. Criteria for optimality of technology management are: for the information technology process is the timeliness of information delivery to managers, its reliability and completeness; for the social technological process - commitment, competence, satisfaction; for the instrumental process - reliability, relevance, capital intensity, capital intensity, productivity.

Information technology in management is aimed at the expedient use of information resources and supplying them with all elements of the organizational structure. Therefore, the degree of using information resources largely determines the effectiveness of the organization.

The sphere of application of modern information technologies in management is very extensive: starting from ensuring the performance of operations for the formation of documents, the organization of electronic document management and ending with system analysis, support for management decisions, and automation of complex corporate systems design. Information technologies cover almost all the main areas of management and are the basis for the development of the informatization process.

1.2. Evolution of Technological Structures

Modern economic conditions are a clear indicator of the change of technological structures and economic structures. In his book "The Third Wave" E. Toffler called these shifts waves. As a rule, all of them are clearly expressed due to social and economic shocks, often accompanied by wars between adherents of old and new ways. In the question under consideration, there are several basic definitions of the ways:

- The new techno-industrial system is a set of fundamentally breakthrough technologies that are tied into a single "multi-techno-system", where the effects of using one technology support the use and development of other technologies;
- Technological structure is a set of technologies characteristic for a certain level of development of production.

We can see from the presented definitions, in essence they are very similar, in fact, the techno-industrial system is the basis of the technological one.

In connection with scientific and technological progress, there is a transition from lower orders to higher, progressive ones. The foundations of the subsequent technological order are, as a rule, born during the period of domination and flourishing of the previous or even pre-previous order. But as long as the previous way does not exhaust all possibilities of its development, the sprouts of the subsequent way are in shadow and do not receive wide development. It is conventionally assumed that the duration of the technological order is 50-60 years.

Strategically breakthrough technologies of a new way are formed not in the framework of specific states and markets, but become supra-territorial forms of education. There are already proposals for the formation of the territory of the New Middle East as opposed to the romantic idea put forward in 1993 by Shimon Peres (1923-2016) of the romantic idea of creating a New Middle East (free of war and based on the harmonious use of all available resources), the basis of which is the matrix of joint development projects Urals, Siberia, Central Asia, the Middle East (from Krasnoyarsk and Yekaterinburg in Russia to India and the Persian Gulf) Pawson R, et al., 2005). The principal difference from the existing examples of economic integration is that a fundamentally new market will be formed on the territory with qualitatively different use of technologies. The industrialization carried out in this territory should already be based on the seventh technological order and create a qualitatively different industrial system. The implementation of such a large-scale project is possible, among other things, due to the lack of technologies for deep processing of natural resources available in the territories represented, which requires the construction of the most advanced productive capacities capable of performing deep processing while simultaneously introducing resources and energy-saving technologies.

The capabilities of individual states to participate in the development of such technologies are not only the basis for controlling the areas under consideration, but, above all, the zone of running in the most advanced technologies, with the aim of discovering and further adapting and developing technologies in their own territories.

In the world economic thought, the issues of technological structures were raised due to the Kondratiev's theory of economic cycles (1982-1938) (Propharma Group, 2019). N. Kondratiev connected the long waves with technical innovations and their own cycles. In the future, the issues of motivations and consequences of scientific and technological progress were fulfilled by J. Schumpeter, K. Freeman, G. Forestester, J. Clark and others (Klein K, et al. 1996, 90-97); Jagosh J, et al. 2011, 99-123).

In the Russian theoretical and practical work the concept of "technological way" was introduced by Russian economists L. Leskov, D. Lvov and S. Glazyev (Beaatriz V., 2017, 88).

According to the global classification used by economists and managers, five existing technological structures are distinguished, manifested to varying degrees in different states. In this case, individual researchers are already talking about the manifestation in the economies of the sixth, and in some cases, even the seventh technological order.

Let us consider in more detail the technological structures' evolution and their basic properties. It should be noticed that the years of their manifestation in economic life are very conditional.

The first technological structure, according to different data, is most relevant to the period 1785-1835s (Berta W, et al., 2005, 234-256); it arose on the basis of the production technologies' development in the textile industry and the extensive use of water energy. Separate examples of developments and applications of steam engines have not been so common. Irrigation canal systems have developed extensively, and roadways have been built for increasing number of delivering goods. Technology of labor organization is changing. There are questions of a competent division of labor, when the allocation of operations according to a predetermined principle makes it possible to increase labor productivity with a similar number of involved resources (Edward de Bono, 2010, 99).

The second technological structure is relating to the period of 1830 – 1890s (Cantwell J, et al., 2013, 345-450). Its main characteristic is the accelerated development of transport and transport infrastructure, as a result, railways and world shipping are developing, which further simplifies the delivery of manufactured products. The development of mechanical production on the basis of a steam engine accelerates the development of light industry, shipbuilding, locomotive building, and extractive industries. Essentially at this stage, production operations were not simply divided, but for the first time the organizers engaged in the specialization of labor in certain areas. This is the next revolution in the field of management technologies.

The third technological order during the period 1880 -1935 was formed under the increase in the possibilities of using electric power, electric distribution networks, the development of communications, including telephone communications. It is during this period that significant changes occur in the organization of production, a new science appears - management (Cohen W, et al., 1990, 45-56). From the point of view of management technologies, they pass to scientifically grounded rails. It becomes important not only due to the competent organization of production processed, but also the concentration within the chain of creation and sale of goods from the first stage, to the final consumption. This leads to the emergence of large monopoly firms (including cartels, syndicates, trusts), which in turn stimulate the concentration of banking and financial capital, including for the purpose of financial support for their activities. If in the previous stages the questions of the organization of production as such were acute, then it is in the third technological order that questions arise about the organization of mass production, and the reduction of the cost of each additional unit.

The fourth technological order of 1930-1990s, appeared as a result of further development of energy using oil and oil products, gas, communications, and new synthetic materials (De Kalbermatten M., 2013, 99). Mass production of cars, tractors, aircraft, various types of weapons, consumer goods appeared and widely distributed computers and software products for them. The atom is used in military and then for peaceful purposes. There is a further change in management technologies, but already at a qualitative level. It is important not just to organize the production of material goods, but in the most effective way. Therefore, the best production and management technologies are adopted by each other by different organizations. Mass production technologies are perceived as the only possible one as a basis for profitability and sustainability of the organization in the long-term period. The only thing that makes changing management technologies is more and more obvious limitations in the availability of resources. If in the previous stages the workers could be treated as cogs of production mechanisms that were absolutely interchangeable, then at this stage social issues are already raised. It is important not only to attract an employee to the production processes, but also to develop it from the standpoint of qualifications and even his own interests. Technology management organizations are also undergoing significant changes. Further development is given to oligopoly competition. There are transnational and transnational companies that make direct investments in the markets of different countries, which are required, including the development of workers in the expanding territories to use the best achievements. This happens through information, social and directly management technologies. Access to information sources is opened; technologies for involving and self-training of workers are developed and tested (including through specialized simulators; for example, training pilots in special capsules, simulating flight conditions, drivers, doctors, etc.).

The fifth technological order of 1985-2035s relies on advances in microelectronics, informatics, biotechnology, genetic engineering, new types of energy, materials, space exploration, satellite communications (Damanpour F, Schneider M., 2006, 88). There is a transition from isolated companies to a single network of large and small companies connected by an electronic network based on the Internet, carrying out close cooperation in the field of technology, product quality control, innovation planning. In the field of control systems in the fifth technological order, they start to move away from large-sized enterprises in favor of medium and small forms. Joint ventures are widely developed. Mass production management technologies create problems to a large extent. Therefore, management technologies become more personalized focused on the production of single, orderly goods and services. In such conditions, the economic effect of mass production is sharply reduced due to a sharp drop in demand for masses (Damanpour F, Schneider M., 2009, 45-78).

1.3. Prospects of Technological Civilization

The transition to the sixth and the beginning transition to the seventh technological order essentially forms a technogenic civilization, which is characterized by dualism, on the one hand, provides humanity with unprecedented opportunities to meet and even create new needs, and on the other, it creates the danger of destroying the foundations of human existence itself. Harmonize these two components, it seems, is possible at the expense of the mentality of a person, which is formed under the influence of technology.

Comprehension of the meaning and role of technology in society began in the XIX - early XX centuries, when the role of engineering environment and technology increased due to the expanding global industrialization. The result was the formulation of two trends: technical optimism and pessimism (Figueiredo P, 2009, 34-39).

Technical optimism is characterized by the idealization of technology, the possibilities of its development, the primary determinative factor of social progress.

Technical pessimism is characterized by denial, demonization and mystification of technology, technology is perceived as the enemy of mankind, the basis of all its troubles (this trend is propagated by technophobes), the basis of inefficient use of financial, human and other resources, including threatening the complete destruction of mankind (the bright representatives of this direction are "cosmophobes") (Frambach R, Schillewaert N., 2002, 78-79).

A bright representative of technological optimism is Henri de Saint-Simon (1760-1825), who was one of the first to notice the trends taking place in society, and singled out in his works as the most significant class of industrialists, on which social justice and equality depends. Through gradual industrialization, from his point of view, not only the rise of the productive force, but also the reform of capitalist society, was to occur (Freemen Chr., Louca Fr., 2001).

Torstein Bund Veblen (1857-1929), who analyzed the subject matter of the technical and cultural process; expressed the idea of mediating the interaction of society and nature with social institutions, some of which are subjects of technical development, while others are neutral (Thumm N., 2004). Subjects of technical development are people who later became known as technocrats. They are representatives of society who belong to the "labor side" in the production of public goods, in its opposition to "idleness" and have distinctive features: the instinct of mastery, the instinct of inquiry and the instinct of self-sacrifice. Veblen criticized the work of A. Sen-Simon for his division of social structures into workers and loafers (Tabak R, et al., 2012). Since traders, artisans and manufacturers in the A. Sen-Simon classification under consideration fell into the category of idlers, and as a result were not so necessary and should have been abolished as a class. At the same time, Veblen's change in the structure of society occurs at the expense of technical workers, who know and determine favorable conditions for the development of technology, who are able to organize the management of society, capable of creating a perfect social mechanism.

Veblen's ideas were supported and developed by John Kenneth Galbraith (1908-2006), who proposed a model for transforming society in the spirit of technical determinism (Selin A., 2007). Developing his theory during the heyday of industrialization, J. Galbraith determined that the factors of production are not equivalent in nature, and the priority among them is given to entrepreneurial talent, since land, capital, and labor can be quite equivalent in industrial society. It is from the holders of the entrepreneurial talent that the opportunities for creating and developing the knowledge necessary for good management depend. Thus, in a developed society, in his opinion, managers are the highest status, whom he calls techno structure. At the same time, this structure is endowed with collective intelligence, which is ahead of the individual's mind. The function of control over the development of society spontaneously passes to the collective entity of technical reality (techno structure) by means of a "silent revolution" or a "revolution of managers".

With technical pessimism, it is generally accepted that, despite the fact that the main factor in the development of society is the level of technology development, which should be socially adapted, and at the same time have the least destructive impact on nature and society (Solomons N, Spross J., 2011, 56-59). The source of this influence is the bearers of the "instrumental mind," i.e, those who try to reduce the mind to the formal structural programs of the operational impact on nature.

Questions for discussion (Chapter 1):

1. What are the main principals of technology management?
2. Which objectives you can submit for modern technological enterprises?
3. What kinds of perspectives for technological entrepreneurship do exist in global market?
4. What is evolution of technology management?
5. What are the main types of technological structures?

Chapter 2

MODERN TRENDS IN TECHNOLOGY DEVELOPMENT

2.1. TECHNOLOGY POLICY IN GLOBAL ENVIRONMENT

Nowadays we have complex modern geo-economic and geopolitical conditions that determine the functioning and self-determination of not only states but also specific enterprises and organizations, their ability to innovate technologically and their commercialization are the basis of competitiveness and sustainability of specific economic entities.

The technological policy of the enterprise (organization) is a set of principles and actions (the way of activity), on the basis of which new products and technological processes are selected, developed and introduced (Sox H., 2010, 470-479).

One can single out the following main tasks of the company's technology policy:

- monitoring of scientific and research achievements in the country and in the world, as well as general technological trends;
- stimulation of constant increase of educational and qualifying level of the company's personnel;

- identification of factors that favor innovation;
- formation of the organizational structure of the enterprise, the most favorable for the implementation of a continuous innovation process, ensuring staff motivation;
- coordination and achievement of actions' coherence of various company's divisions on carrying out of research and development (Roger M., 2003, 89).

The constant growth of the technology's role in the development of national economies makes us pay special attention to the activities of large corporations. Greater demands are placed on the processes of organizing production operations and increasing their efficiency within international companies, and primarily industrial enterprises; since it is from them that the ability to implement the developed strategies and ensure the competitiveness of enterprises depends, the performance of all necessary activities is better than competitors (Roger M., 2004, 45-57).

Operational efficiency is not limited to efficiency and timeliness of the production functions performed within the enterprise, aimed at satisfying consumers. Factors should be considered such as quality, reduction of marriage and constant improvement of products, that is, the perfection of management and production technologies. As pointed out by R. Kaplan and D. Northan without well-established production management it is impossible to implement a strategy, even if it is a strategy not related to achieving the structure of the lowest costs in the industry (Feldstein A, Glasgow R., 2011, 123-134).

We cannot disagree with the statements made by M. Porter, that it is impossible to infinitely increase operational efficiency as a basis for the stability of competitive advantages, because competitors, using only control and production technologies, some equipment suppliers, sooner or later come to the same level of operational efficiency.

As a result, the only strategy for the functioning, further development and individualization of the business entity in the market is one that takes into account and reflects all its features. At the same time, it is interesting to note M. Porter's remark that "competition based exclusively on operational efficiency is mutually destructive and leads to debilitating wars, which can be stopped only by limiting competition" (Fixsen D, et al., 2005, 56-67). Restricting competition, leads to monopolization of the market, which in turn leads to the hegemony of large international companies.

Thus, the development of technology acts as the main driving force of the company's economic growth.

2.2. Types and Forms of Technology Policy

The policy of the global corporation's CEO is to find new technologies in the home country to create new products and processes, using the centralized resources of the parent company, and to spread innovation around the world offices of MNCs (European Innovation Scoreboard, 2008). However, recently more and more companies are inclined to the polycentric policy, in various forms of its manifestation.

Centralization of R&D is due to the following reasons:

- the need for deep secrecy and control by MNE management over technology, which is seen as a long-term competitive advantage;
- the need for close interaction between the development of documentation and equipment and, subsequently, between the functions of production and the development of technology;
- in a rapidly changing competitive environment, centralization reduces the time for R&D;
- facilitates the simplification in the accumulation of funds needed to finance development;
- facilitates simplification in communication with external investors and partners (Gallivan M., 2001, 203-209).

However, with the policy of the global center, certain risks arise, which are related to the difficulties of introducing new technology in subsidiaries; the lack of local requirements and other problems of rigid centralization. As a rule, companies that use this type of technological policy are distinguished by the fact that in the countries of the global center the state creates conditions under which it is profitable to engage in innovative business. These conditions include: state funding for science, education and innovation, focused on the absorption and improvement of imported technologies to create their own innovations in the absence of a private sector, capable of commercializing new ideas, the whole process is targeted. In addition, major production sites are large production complexes (can be products and programs), imported initially, integrate the efforts of researchers, engineers, technologists, as a result, contribute to the diversification of production and the intensification of production of innovative products. As a result, such a policy of the state in the country creates a critical mass of knowledge and competencies, as a result of which the entire innovation system passes to a higher level of development (for example, Japan) (Global Innovation Index report, 2018).

The policy of polycentrism is increasingly being used, which suggests that MNC's subsidiaries use their own capabilities and resources to develop new technologies that provide their own needs. This model allows reflecting the unique needs of different countries in which MNEs operate, as well as the possibilities of interaction with suppliers.

Earlier, the legendary DuPont research center in Wilmington (Delaware) gave out new product development (nylon, viscose, teflon), now R&D is engaged in small groups focused closer to emerging markets. They work with regional requests, use local developments and know-how. Hempel's chief operating officer, Lars Peterson, states that they are trying to find the ideal balance between a centralized R&D organization, focusing on the global market and local challenges and customer needs in specific areas (Greenhalgh T, et al., 2004, 89-98).

However, it is necessary to understand that this type of technological policy also has a number of negative sides that are nevertheless leveled by modern information technologies:

- there is a high probability of increasing the aspirations of national branches to autonomy;
- increased likelihood of duplication of developments already carried out in other subsidiaries in cases where each local branch is looking for a solution to the problem;
- occurrence of additional costs for R&D;
- the emergence of additional costs for the registration of patents in different countries of the company's presence.

Due to the fact that during the implementation of the technology policy, MNE managers should create conditions for expanding the opportunities for the spread of transnational innovations to the latter: “locally-leveraged” (distributed technology development system) and “globally-linked” (integrated system of technological development) (Godin G, et al., 2008, 88-98).

Local-leveraged technology includes using the resources of the national office to create innovations not only for the local market, but also for distributing them on a worldwide basis. This allows the management of MNCs to combine the innovative resources of all subsidiaries and use them for the entire corporation. MNC is able to respond to market changes that occur in one country and use them to identify similar trends in other countries. This method of carrying out the technological policy requires management to develop and supervise the process of training the personnel of the daughter companies of the corporation, to coordinate their activities in the field of R&D, but it enables the company to significantly increase the efficiency of the use of innovative resources.

However, local innovations developed by one country office are not always easily transferred to other branches. The main obstacles are attempts to transfer products or processes that do not meet the conditions of another country; lack of coordination of transfer mechanisms; in the barriers defined by the syndrome “is not done here”, which manifests itself in the struggle of national branches for conducting their own autonomous research and development (Glasgow R, et al., 2003, 309-345).

A technology policy such as "globally-linked" involves pooling the resources and capabilities of all MNC divisions both at the parent company level and at the level of subsidiaries for joint creation and implementation of innovations (Glasgow R., 2003, 88). Using unique scientifically patented developments and resources, globally-linked technologies are developing qualitatively new technologies, with the possibility of increasing not only the efficiency but also the effectiveness of the developments. Creating the same flexible organizational links, including the construction of strategic alliances, allows the efforts of many units to unite to achieve a synergistic effect in the use of their resources.

In any case, the type of technology policy should be selected for the specific goals and objectives of the organization, because a non-relevant policy can only bring negative instead of a positive effect, up to the termination of the organization's activities. When choosing a technology policy, it is necessary to remember that innovations and changes should not be an end in itself, but only an increase in the efficiency of functioning and the creation of favorable conditions, including for the growth of the value of human capital and the activation of the creative activity of its employees.

2.3. Internationalization of Technology Policy

Let us understand the technological methods as simplification of the product's adaptation to regional linguistic and cultural features there is different from the place of development, from the Latin "Inter" between the nation and the nation, it acts as a "proactive modernization tool" that stimulates "A successful existence in the context of globalization" (Garland A, et al., 2010, 243-256).

However, recently there has been a process of "ethnization", which is associated with an increase in the influx of refugees to Europe from the countries of the Middle East; to Russia - from countries of the post-Soviet space (Graham I., Logan J., 2004, 354-367). Let us consider in detail these processes.

After the "Arab revolution" of 2011, which occurred in the countries of the Middle East and Africa, a flow of refugees poured into the EU countries (Main Science & Technology Indicators (MSTI), 2019). The main problem is not even in the number of migrants arriving in the EU countries, but in the socio-cultural difference in perceptions of the world around them, attitudes toward problems of sexism, needs for work, welfare requirements, etc.

Emerging "newcomers" are in cultural to the local population, differ in language, appearance, religion, they can hardly adapt to local peculiarities, bring their own habits, manners, way of life and lifestyle, models of social organization, unusual or even alien to the local population, manifest in in turn, inhospitality.

As a consequence, there is a high probability of a struggle for economic and symbolic resources, including in a very aggressive form.

The intensity of inflow of migrants leads to the appearance of ethnically marked elements (signboards, inscriptions, design elements, housing concentration). The result is a modification of the basic approach to the internationalization of business, when new rules for doing business in local markets are developed, significantly different from the classical ones.

These changes due to the functioning of TNCs require a rethinking of the main provisions of the ideas of the theory of market power of St. Heimer and the theory of internalization (Urban development: innovation plus the potential of cities, 2018). The main problem is that the basic provisions imply the possibility of free circulation on the market of unique assets of companies undergoing changes. Since, in some cases, there is no possibility of separating assets from a company that owns them without a significant change in value. As a result, the possibility of transferring unique characteristics of companies abroad is questioned.

In cases where the market situation is not considered within the framework of the internationalization approach as the main and the properties of the company itself are paramount, and the process of their creation, the development of remote divisions of TNCs, according to the classics of the internationalization approach, is due to the accumulation of knowledge related to the development process and the ability to transfer human capital within the organization. One of the first to point out the importance of human capital in the dissemination of technological knowledge was R. Vernon, who noted the existence of migration trends in production capacities from highly-developed countries to countries with cheap labor as the product progressed within the life cycle (Valente T., 1996, 79); (WIPO Statistics Database: Statistics on Patents, 2019). Initially, the product, in his opinion, is innovative, requires for the production of a unique technology that exists only in the home market of the company that developed the product. The demand of foreign consumers at the first stages of the life cycle is met through the export of the product. In the future, production is transferred to countries with the greatest technological potential. But as soon as the development of technology reaches the stage of standardization, companies are forced to move production to less developed countries, since in this case there is a need to minimize labor costs. In the context of significant refugee migration flows, it was assumed that there might be economies of scale for TNCs by preserving production processes in the home countries and replacing the labor force with a newcomer. However, practice has shown that under the conditions of ethnization the R. Vernon theory under consideration does not work and requires a substantial rethinking (World receipts of royalties and license fees by region, 2009 and 2010).

Questions for discussion (Chapter 2):

1. What are the main elements of internalization?
2. Which global factors affect technology policy?
3. What kind of trends do MNC and TNC have in technology policy?
4. What is classification of technology policy?
5. What are the main tasks of technology policy?

Chapter 3

GLOBAL ENVIRONMENT FOR INNOVATIONS

3.1. STRUCTURE AND LEVELS OF GLOBAL ENVIRONMENT

The relative importance of various factors of economic growth has evolved over time, and to date, for an increasing number of countries, innovations in their many manifestations are becoming a leading factor in economic growth. Among the countries, with the increased and constantly increasing role of the level of innovative development, is Russia. So, innovations are given the leading role in the transformation of society and the economy of the country, which corresponds to the theories of Schumpeter (Schumpete J. 1982, 56-58), Mensch (Mitchell S, et al., 2010, 87-98), Kondratiev (Meyer A, Goes J., 1988, 290-305), Kuznets (Marcus H. 2012, 98-123); these ideas are developed in the research works of different nations researchers.

The global environment in economic field may be divided into 3 main areas:

1. Micro environment (markets and economic members which surround company in domestic market);
2. Macro environment (at least one international market, political, economic, technological factors in different markets);

3. Global environment (all markets are considered as one global market, global factors: ecological, innovative, and social).

In the modern economy there is a concept of a “new economy”, which has recently been subject to disapproving discussions by critics, but still not enough arguments have been found to reject this concept. It is necessary to clarify the main points of this concept. So, in the report “The state of the world in 2001”, the main components of the concept “new economy” were defined. First, it is the new base of the entire economy, where the raw material is information; Secondly, these are modern sources of energy - electronics and semiconductors; thirdly, radically new sources of information transfer - information systems (Gupta N, Healey D., 2013, 45-78). The main tool of this economy is information penetrating into all spheres not only economic, but also social, political life of society. This concept does not force and does not limit the economy to this concept; on the contrary, it provides an opportunity for further development in all sectors where information and communication technologies also remain at the core.

The main characteristics of global environment nowadays are:

1. Competitiveness,
2. Flexibility,
3. Development,
4. Social orientation,
5. Advanced technology,
6. Cooperation,
7. Knowledge transferring,
8. Transferring of innovations.

At the current stage of development, it is possible to determine the main characteristics of the modern economy.

1. Globalization is one of the laws of the development in the modern world. This concept applies not only to the economic sphere of society. For the economy as a whole, this process is superior to the

integration process. Globalization involves interaction between people, companies, and states of different countries by means of world trade and investment, where information technologies are also based. To date, there has been an increase in the scale and pace of capital movements, which creates a single space for economic activity. Strict price and non-price competition is observed, which gives a strong impetus to the development of innovations in the country. Thus, it is possible to single out the main aspects of the influence of the process of globalization on innovative development:

2. Acceleration of the pace of production of new technologies. Due to the severe competition and the continuous release of new products (technologies, inventions, services, and various consumer goods), a short period of time remains for the creation and realization of new ideas. This development is also based on information and communication technologies. As a result, the "life" of each product has significantly decreased, because something is constantly being created [1, pp. 23-56].
3. Inter-firm cooperation and development of network organizational structures. Products obtained at the output after productions are the result of the action of integration interactions of various technologies. Due to the short life cycle of a modern product, even the largest companies are unable to conduct high-quality and large-scale information research and quickly enter the arena of world markets. This encourages organizations (even large ones) to cooperate in the field of information research, and as a result, there is an increase in growth and stimulation of networking between enterprises.
4. Functional integration and cooperation within enterprises. The presence of flexible horizontal links between the managerial and research links in the company can ensure rapid integration of world trends, which again is necessary for the rapid creation and successful implementation of a new product.

5. Cooperation with centers of knowledge production. It implies close cooperation with state laboratories, research universities, and centers of applied and academic science:
   - Increase in the share of services and the role of knowledge transfer. This process encourages companies to use outsourcing as a new way of organizing economic activity, which allows you to achieve certain years and savings. Also, this affects the change in existing business models, since the implementation of interaction between companies requires a higher level of organization.
   - High level of importance of intellectual capital. This characterizes the fact that there is an increase in the importance of value added from the intangible assets of the enterprise and the intellectual capital. One of the first authors who paid attention to this trend was J. Tobin, who said that this leads to a significant excess of the value of their capitalization over the level of the value of tangible assets (Hayati B, 2019). This means that the level of intellectual capital is the most important for the shareholders of companies.
   - Increase in entrepreneurial activity. This characteristic speaks of the increased activity of small entrepreneurs, moreover, in most developed countries; the creation of favorable conditions for the "existence" of small entrepreneurs is a priority task of the state strike. So, in the USA for the last 20 years 90% of jobs were created by small entrepreneurs, whereas the number of jobs of large corporations has decreased on the contrary (Hoffman, K., et al. 1998, 67-90). The increase in entrepreneurial activity in recent years is characteristic of all developed countries.

The described characteristics (Figure 1) of a modern or new economy allow us to say about the importance of creation, development (dissemination) and application of new knowledge (Hamel G., et al., 2005, 390-401). The qualitative functioning of these data characterizes the successful course of economic development. Thus, the above-mentioned fact was confirmed that the basis of the modern economy is information that takes various forms, like knowledge, technology, experience and other possible forms of obtaining and processing information. The qualitative functioning of the economy at all levels is determined by the level of ability to apply and develop new knowledge, through which the innovative activity of the economy increases.

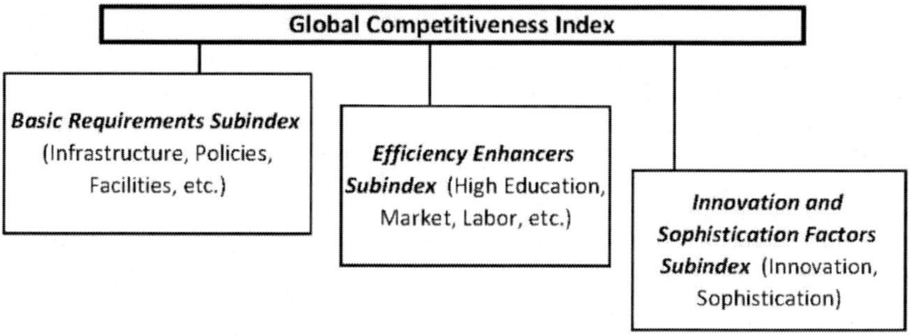

Source: Horwitz S, Chamberlain P, Landsverk J, Mullican C. (2010) Improving the Mental Health of Children in Child Welfare Through the Implementation of Evidence-Based Parenting Interventions. Administration and Policy in Mental Health and Mental Health Services Research; 37(1-2), pp. 27-39. doi: 10.1007/s10488-010-0274-3.

Figure 1. Structure of global competitive index.

In a modern economy with constantly growing competition and the level of innovation, more and more companies are faced with non-price problems. Now it is more important not only to have skills, but to have the potential to receive and effectively introduce new knowledge (skills). Thus, the source of the value is shifted; knowledge occupies a leading position instead of labor.

4. Permanent increase in the rate of economic growth. This process has a long enough character, since the 1970s there has been a long increase, not counting economic crises, which also subsequently gave impetus for further recovery after the economic recovery. The reason for this trend is the increased level of technology development and increase in the level of

profitability, as well as the active injection of large amounts of investment. The increase in the rates of economic growth is accompanied by the strengthening of the role of the state and the development of a clear and stable macro policy by the majority of developed and developing countries. Moreover, most of the state budget is directed to the development of human capital, which indicates the desire to raise the level of production. Financing of educational institutions, professional training and retraining of working cadres and scientific development centers is increasing. Concerning South Korea, a reorientation of domestic-oriented enterprises takes place in accordance with the trends in the development of global production. The table shows an increase in the costs of education (Table 2). In South Korea, the cost of education increased to 74,317 million US dollars, most of the costs are spent to research activities.

Table 2. Educational costs in different countries, 2012-2015

Country	Educational costs (mln dollars USA)			
	2012	2013	2014	2015
USA	925 712	984 192	1 053 000	1 093 000
France	131 528	132 678	138 377	141 421
Italy	56 575	64 581	60 532	63 353
Germany	158 567	164 442	171 861	181 287
Great Britain	96 293	104 451	109 392	117 101
South Korea	26 599	34 402	44 597	55 921

Source: J.H. Kim and J.H. Han Differentiated Effects of Product Strategy and CEO Characteristics on Venture Firms` Growth: The Moderating Role of Organizational Life Cycle Stage. Journal of Technology Innovation, 22(1), 2014.

To date, as already indicated in the main factors of the modern economy, the role of education, that is, the teaching economy has increased. Under the economy in this case, we understand the training not only of individuals, but of firms in general. In the conditions of tough competition and constant changes in the market (the emergence of various trends), the ability of the firm not only to change the level of individual skills, but also the opportunity to reorganize the firm (the technological and organizational structure of the enterprise) becomes actual. Against this backdrop, the role of the economy that plays the role of the educator is growing. Learning economy (learning economy) is a model of an economy in which the ability to learn is a decisive factor for the economic success of individual enterprises, regions and countries (Lakshminarayanan A, 2019, 478-487). It is important to note that this economy does not imply the use of high technologies; on the contrary, training is possible in low-tech industries. Perhaps only a difference between the potentials of different sectors, but in either case there is a niche in each of them with a high level of potential for training.

3.2. RISK MANAGEMENT IN INTERNATIONAL BUSINESS

It would be fair to note that risk management in international business, first of all, implies their prevention. To do this, you need to know what "pitfalls" await the beginner in this area. In fact, nothing fundamentally new has been invented recently; we will only spread out the information "on the shelves" (Lerner, J. and Wulf, J., 2007, 56-78).

Unfortunately, not all risks can be foreseen or influence their prevention. These include natural disasters, the political situation in the world, the economic situation in the country in which the branch/ representative office is opened.

Depending on the ability to influence the current situation, experts identify unprofitable, partially amenable and amenable factors of economic risks.

Management of economic risks in international business is not possible, if it is an external enterprise environment. Partial influence can be exerted on consumer demand. Full control over risks is available only in the internal sphere of the company:

- raise the quality of products,
- regulate the cost price,
- increase the core competences of personnel.

Risk control is an important part of effective international trading activity. Quality control implies constant monitoring and compliance with the rules of the established strategy, in order to reduce the consequences of risks to a minimum. In the economy there are established and generally accepted risk management techniques that organizations face. These include:

- Organization of production technology,
- Planning,
- Control over the execution of production terms and quality,
- Forecasting and analysis.

Before applying a new development strategy or moving to a new stage, especially as entering foreign markets, it is necessary to calculate and compare the potential income received and potentially incurred costs and risks. If the first shows a significant advantage, then the risk is justified, if not - it is better to delay with the extension or choose another option.

In the sphere of foreign economic activity, the emergence of economic risks is possible both in normal commercial transactions and in international investment and credit relations related to capital investment and the deployment of financial (currency) resources (Levin R., et al., 1987, 167-189). Thus, the concepts of uncertainty and risk in an excellent degree refer to the sphere of national and international business. Managers of international company must make daily decisions about sales, purchases, organization of work of production and other divisions of the firm. At the same time, they face changing market conditions in the international markets, competitors' actions, changing consumer preferences, environmental constraints, traditions and specifics of doing business, specific national and international legislation, and other factors. Moreover, the complication of economic practices, expansion beyond national borders makes it critical to take into account risk and uncertainty in international business.

Thus, the risks of international business are understood as possible unfavorable events that may occur and as a result of which it is potentially possible to incur losses, property damage to a participant in foreign economic activity. Risks related to foreign economic activity are divided into two groups: internal, or dependent on the activities of the enterprise, and external, or independent of the activities of the enterprise (Figure 2).

The principal difference between the two main groups of risks is that the enterprise is able to influence the first group of risks, i.e., take measures that eliminate the sources of these risks; the company cannot affect the second group of risks, since their offensive practically does not depend on its efforts.

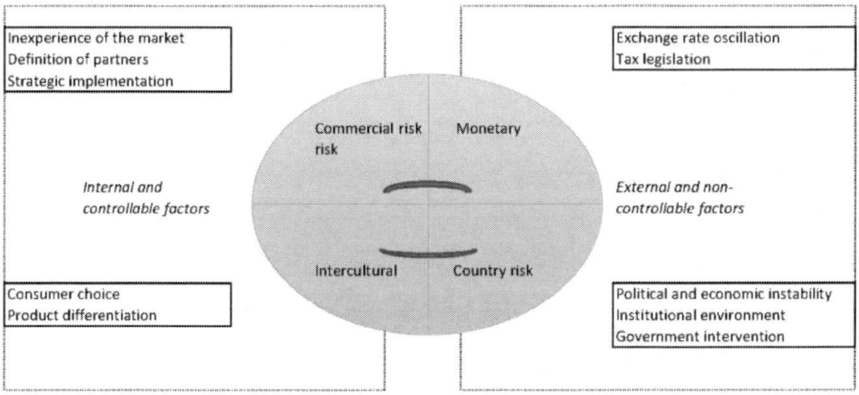

Source: author's survey.

Figure 2. Classification of risks in international trade activities.

Consider risk groups in accordance with this classification.

As we have determined, internal risks include the following:

1. risks associated with economic activity;
2. technical and technological risks;
3. production risk;
4. risks related to the human factor.

Risks related to economic activity (production, transport, trade, financial, etc.). These are risks associated with the conduct of business activities and the results of economic processes.

Before entering foreign markets, managers need to calculate and match potential income and potential costs and risks of the business.

When switching to foreign economic activity, first of all, it is necessary to focus on external risks: the company cannot exert influence on them. International practice identifies several groups that are able to significantly reduce losses from potential risks:

1. Insurance.

   Using of bank guarantees, collateral, availing's and other. These forms of settlement-credit manipulation allow reducing the risk of non-payment for shipped goods or the cancellation of the delivery of already paid goods.
2. Hedging.

   Analysis and drawing up a plan for the external market conjuncture that you are targeting. This includes: the study of prices, the level of consumer demand in relation to offers. This allows to identify potential risks when entering the market and to avoid them as much as possible.

Other methods: the effect of compensation, the distribution and localization of risk, evasion from it.

3.3. External Innovative Environment Analysis

The modern economy, it seems to us, has a determining factor, namely innovations, which allows us to use the term "innovation economy" (Lotti F., Santarelli E. and Vivarelli M., 2009, 456-467).

An innovative economy is an economy dominated by the innovation-based management principle, the essence of which is that science and education are beginning to be the main source of various innovations.

Technical and scientific progress, which has been carried out for a long time in parallel, is the only direction in development in the innovative economy.

In every country that chooses an innovative way of development, the organization of innovation has different manifestations (Table 3). These discrepancies depend on the political standing of the country, on the institutions involved in this innovative activity. Due to this, different manifestations of the construction of an innovative economy are possible.

Table 3. The evolution of entrepreneurship

Category	Step		
	pre-industrial	industrial	post-industrial
Area	Arbitrage trade (work on the difference of certain indicators depending on the time)	Material production	Intangible production, innovation
Role	Auxiliary	Increase	Leading
Concept	Search for areas of profitable capital application	Finding the best combination of factors	Innovation
Function	Monopoly of the owner (sole proprietor)	Dispersal of the owner's monopoly (corporation)	The specialization of production, instead of adapting to the external conditions of their transformation

Source: Author's survey.

In recent years, the world has witnessed the power of innovation and its various constituents in revolutionizing the business and economic landscape. With the advancement of the knowledge economy, the world is also seeing how innovation empowers individuals, communities and countries with profound impact on business, politics, and society. What is equally evident is the increasing role that innovation plays in accelerating economic growth and promoting development.

Innovation has proved to be a key enabler of progress and competitiveness; especially in times when the world is recovering from the aftershocks of a global recession. Today, with the focus worldwide on stabilizing the global economy and jumpstarting growth, a strong emphasis on directed pro-innovation policies can be a rainbow of hope for nations worldwide.

For evaluation global innovation ability many countries try to find their rank inside global innovation index system.

The Global Innovation Index (GII) aims to capture the multi-dimensional facets of innovation and provide the tools that can assist in tailoring policies to promote long-term output growth, improved productivity, and job growth. The GII helps to create an environment in which innovation factors are continually evaluated. It provides a key tool and a rich database of detailed metrics for economies, which in 2017 encompasses 127 economies, representing 92.5% of the world's population and 97.6% of global GDP (Global Innovation Index report, 2018) (Figure 3).

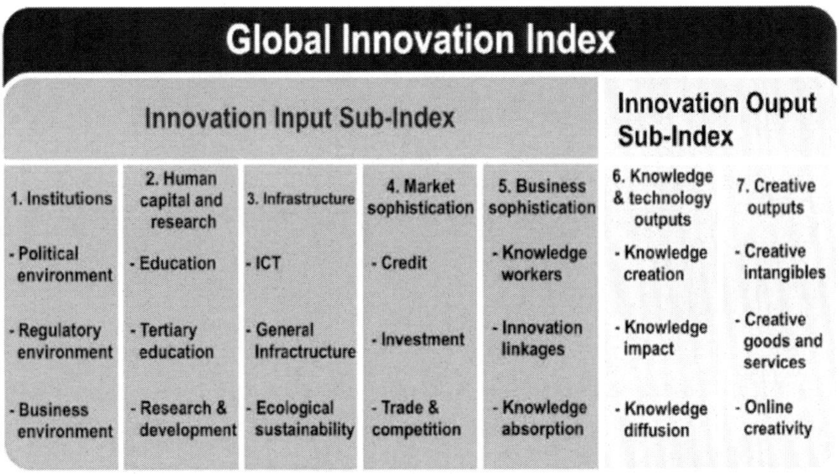

Source: https://www.globalinnovationindex.org/

Figure 3. Structure of Global Innovation Index.

The Global Innovation Index 2018 (GII), in its 11th edition this year, was released June 15, and continued to be co-published by Cornell University, INSEAD, and the World Intellectual Property Organization (WIPO, an agency of the United Nations) (WIPO Statistics Database:

Statistics on Patents, 2018). The core of the GII Report consists of a ranking of world economies' innovation capabilities and results. Over the last ten years, the GII has established itself as a leading reference on innovation. Understanding in more detail the human aspects behind innovation is essential for the design of policies that help promote economic development and richer innovation-prone environments locally. Recognizing the key role of innovation as a driver of economic growth and prosperity, and the need for a broad horizontal vision of innovation applicable to developed and emerging economies, the GII includes indicators that go beyond the traditional measures of innovation such as the level of research and development.

The Global Innovation Index (GII) is an evolving project that builds on its previous editions while incorporating newly available data and that is inspired by the latest research on the measurement of innovation. The GII relies on two sub-indices - the Innovation Input Sub-Index and the Innovation Output Sub-Index - each built around key pillars.

Five input pillars capture elements of the national economy that enable innovative activities: (1) Institutions, (2) Human capital and research, (3) Infrastructure, (4) Market sophistication, and (5) Business sophistication. Two output pillars capture actual evidence of innovation outputs: (6) Knowledge and technology outputs and (7) Creative outputs.

Each pillar is divided into sub-pillars and each sub-pillar is composed of individual indicators (81 in total in 2017). Sub-pillar scores are calculated as the weighted average of individual indicators; pillar scores are calculated as the weighted average of sub-pillar scores.

Four measures are then calculated:

- Innovation input Sub-Index: is the simple average of the first five pillar scores.
- Innovation output Sub-Index is the simple average of the last two pillar scores.
- The overall GII score is the simple average of the input and output Sub-Indices.

- The Innovation Efficiency Ratio is the ratio of the output Sub-Index over the input Sub-Index.

The GII gathers data from more than 30 sources, covering a large spectrum of innovation drivers and results; privileging hard data over qualitative assessments (for example, only five survey questions were included in the GII 2017 report).

In the case when innovative economic relations become the dominant factor in the development of the economic system, it is transformed into an innovative economic system. The beginning of innovative economic activity is an innovative idea.

Questions for discussion (Chapter 3):

1. What are the main elements of global environment?
2. Which global factors influence on economic behavior of business?
3. What kind of risk can be met in global economy?
4. What is classification of international markets?
5. What are the main trends in global innovations?

Chapter 4

INNOVATIVE ENTREPRENEURSHIP IN GLOBAL MARKETS

4.1. INTERNATIONAL INDUSTRIAL MARKETS

The transition to a continuous innovation process is an important feature of modern economic growth. Conducting R&D takes an increasing weight in investment spending, exceeding in science-intensive industries costs for the acquisition of equipment and construction in global environment (Williams C. and Lee S., 2009, 167-178).

The innovation process is the process of transforming scientific knowledge into innovation, which can be represented as a succession of events, during which the innovation ripens from the idea to a specific product, technology or service and is distributed in practical use (Tan J., 2016, 99-134).

In the innovation process, companies are dealing with the application to economic practice or the involvement in the economic circulation of new or otherwise used knowledge, which in itself is a new knowledge of the use of old knowledge. It is logical to assert that the effectiveness of the innovation process is directly related to the effectiveness of "involving" new knowledge in economic practice (Stetler C., 2001, 89-99). From this point of view, the concepts of "technology transfer" and "diffusion of innovations" stand out in the theory of innovations.

International markets are now considered (1) either from a competition point of view for the most significant resources, (2) either from the standpoint of competition for the consumer, (3) or from the position of competition for the territorial-regional presence.

The classification of international markets is based on their composition, distinctive features:

1. international competitive market:
    - developed market,
    - developing market,
    - border market;
2. international market of products and services:
    - world financial market,
    - international market of innovations,
    - world information services market,
    - international technology market;
3. international resource market:
    - world mineral and raw materials market,
    - international labor market.

The international market is a legal, economic and managerial relationship between the subjects of productive activities outside the state, which include foreign sellers, government agencies, producers, suppliers and consumers of goods, services and resources. The international market (from the point of view of competition) is an integral part of national (internal) markets, directly connected with the markets of other countries that are in constant competition. The international market is an integral element of the world market, which is a community of national markets in general, and not their specific parts.

The international competition market is the economic and legal relationships of market entities aimed at forming the leading competitive advantages in the struggle for the consumer, resource or territorial presence.

The world commodity market is an area of commodity-money relations between states that are based on the international division of labor.

The world financial market is a set of national and international markets that ensure the direction, accumulation and redistribution of monetary capital between market participants through financial institutions in order to achieve a normal balance between supply and demand for capital.

The world market of information services is a set of information, international economic and legal relations based primarily on the use of information technology, between the main actors operating within a transboundary space and exchanging products and services.

The international market of innovations is a set of international market relations arising in the process of creation, development, transfer and use of technologies, goods and services at the intercountry level. On the international innovation market, not only finished products can be presented, but also unfinished intellectual products.

The international technology market is the sphere of international trade associated with the purchase and sale of technological solutions: licenses, patents, projects and documentation.

The international resource market is the socioeconomic relations of market entities in the field of extraction, processing, development and trade of tangible and intangible resources with a view to obtaining benefits.

The world (international) labor market is a system of relations that develops between states on the coordination of labor supply and supply, regulation of its interstate flows, remuneration of labor and social protection in the context of international interaction of national economies.

The world mineral and raw materials market is a market where the leading raw materials are initiated by the world's leading and exporters and importers.

Classification of markets is a key parameter in assessing their investment climate. Consulting company MSCI annually in its studies seeks to establish a balance between the level of economic development of the country and the availability of its market, maintaining the stability of the index (Sul Ch., 2008, 44-56). MSCI also presented its own classification of international markets, tied, however, to their regional presence.

The classification structure of MSCI markets consists of the following three criteria:

- the economic development of the country,
- the size and liquidity of its market institutions, and access to markets.

To be classified, a country must meet the requirements of all three criteria. The criterion of economic development is used only in defining the classification of developed markets, while the difference between developing and border markets gives a very wide variety. The size and liquidity requirements are based on the minimum investment opportunity requirements for MSCI; the analysis takes into account global standard indices.

According to MSCI, access to the markets is more interested in international institutional investors, and as a result, the criteria for market access include several sub-criteria. These criteria are usually based on the analysis of qualitative measures (changes in investment policy, structure of foreign investment, etc.), which are considered for all markets annually. Emerging markets are economies that are in the process of rapid development and industrialization, often offering great potential for economic and political growth. Various financial and economic authorities qualify emerging markets on widely varying criteria. Many researchers say that the category of developing countries can include any country that has not yet been mastered in terms of international exchange and trade, but is now still in the process of development on financial, political, and social platforms.

4.2. Technology Transferring in Global Markets

According to the official recommendations of the Organization for Economic Cooperation and Development (OECD) to some global corporations, which are cold "The proposed standard practice for surveys, research and experimental development", technology transfer is the transfer of scientific and technical knowledge and experience for the provision of scientific and technical services, production output (OECD, "Reviews of Innovation Policy: Korea", 2018).

Let's discuss different types of innovation transferring. The technology transfer is divided into commercial and non-commercial.

Commercialization of technology (commercial transfer) is an element of a transfer in which a consumer (buyer) pays a reward to the owner (which may or may not be a developer) of technology in one form or another, determined by mutually agreed contractual terms. Commercial forms of technology transfer include licensing agreements, engineering, contracts and subcontracts for joint R&D and production cooperation (including the creation of joint ventures), investment and other types of agreements related to the assignment, transfer and protection of intellectual and industrial property rights.

The objects of commercial technology transfer are:

- objects of industrial property (patents for inventions, industrial design certificates and utility models), with the exception of trademarks, service marks and commercial names, if they are not part of technology transfer transactions;
- know-how and technical experience in the form of feasibility studies, models, samples, instructions, drawings, specifications, tooling and tools, consultancy services and training;
- technical and technological knowledge and information.

Commercial technology transfer is usually implemented at the 2nd - 5th stages of the innovation process.

In turn, the diffusion of scientific and technical knowledge and information, in contrast to the commercialization of technology, is a non-profit element of the transfer of scientific and technological achievements. This method is realized either in those cases when the owner of scientific and technical knowledge does not have the opportunity or is not interested in its commercialization, or in cases when knowledge itself, being fundamental, basic, is not subject to commercialization. For example, according to the electronic dictionaries "Glossary.ru" and "Wikipedia", diffusion is "the dissemination and adoption of innovations, information, elements of culture and other objects in the social system".

The objects of non-commercial technology transfer are:

- scientific and technical and educational literature, reference books, reviews of standards, patent descriptions, catalogs of prospectuses, etc.;
- international conferences, symposia, exhibitions;
- training of scientists and specialists on a gratuitous basis or on a parity basis for reimbursement of expenses by the parties.

As for the diffusion of innovations, this is the stage of the innovation process, during which the mass dissemination of materialized knowledge in the form of new products or technologies obtained at the previous stages of the innovation process.

Diffusion of innovation is the process through which innovation spreads through communication channels in time and space among participants in the social system.

The objects of innovation diffusion are:

- a new or improved product;
- a new or improved technological process.

As for the commercial and non-commercial transfer of technology, its object is knowledge and information obtained at the stage of R&D, rather than a specific materialized new technology or a new product.

Thus, it is necessary to clearly distinguish such concepts as "technology transfer" and "diffusion of innovations", because these processes have completely different objects.

To date, it is impossible to quantify the amount of international technology transfer due to the ambiguity of its understanding, the lack of reliable and comparable statistics. But we can state an increase in scientific and practical interest in this problem. After all, there is an understanding that an international transfer of technology is one of the directions of modernization and transfer of global economy to an innovative development path.

The main difference between the technology package and the technology itself is that it enables not only to identify the transfer objects and take into account the financial flows for them, but also to characterize the degree of technological development of production, industry, and the country. Thus, in the case of an international transfer of technology in the industry with high added value, transfer of relevant experience, knowledge, objects of intellectual property (OIP) and high technology goods and services will be observed, and with low added value transfer of relevant elements of the technology package.

It is known that the leaders of international technology transfer are transnational corporations (TNCs), which in 2012 accounted for about 97% of world exports of OIP (World Bank report, 2018). In the process of international technology transfer within TNCs the following interrelations are formed:

- the transfer of technologies from the parent company to its affiliated foreign structures;
- transfer between affiliated companies within the corporate network;
- transfer from affiliated foreign companies to the parent company in the home country.

As a result, there are bilateral vertical and horizontal relationships between companies in the corporate structure of TNCs. In the case of interaction between the parent company and affiliated structures, vertical ties take place; and between foreign affiliated firms within the TNCs there are horizontal links.

The main streams of foreign exchange earnings from exports of North American OIP were distributed as follows: technology of production processes - 35%, software - 31.7%, trademarks - 12.7%, franchise - 4.4%. The share of copyright (books, audio and video recordings, documentary) accounts for 16.2% of all foreign exchange earnings from OIP exports. Foreign currency payments for the use of foreign OIP were channeled into production process technologies (56.2%), software (19.7%), trademarks (13.4%), franchises (0.8%); objects of copyright (9.9%) (Table 4) (World Development Indicators report, 2014).

Table 4. The volume of foreign exchange earnings from the exports of North American OIP to the regions (2011), billion US dollars

Country	Total	OIP						
		Production technologies	Books, audio/video records	Documents	Franchising	Trademarks	IT (license)	other
USA	105,6	35,8	15,2	0,6	4,6	14,1	35,0	0,3
Canada	8,3	2,1	1,4	0,02	1,1	0,9	2,8	0,05
EU	52,3	19,8	9,3	0,3	1,6	7,6	13,6	0,1
Latin America	11,9	3,5	1,3	0,1	0,5	1,4	5,0	0,04
Africa	1,0	0,2	0,1	**	**	0,3	0,3	0,007
Middle East	0,9	0,2	0,2	*	0,1	0,1	0,2	0,1
Asia	31,3	10,1	2,7	0,2	1,1	3,9	13,2	0,1
Global Corporations	0,001	*	0	0	0	*	0	0

Notes:

* Less than 500 thousand US dollars.

** No data available.

Source: World receipts of royalties and license fees by region, 2009 and 2010//World Trade Organization [Electronic resource]. - 2011. - Mode of access: http://www.wto.org/english/res_e/statis_e/its2011_e/its11_trade_category_e.htm. - Date of access: 01.04.2017.

TNCs also take part in organizing the activities of joint ventures, in mergers and acquisitions, strategic alliances to implement/gain new competitive advantages and acquire new competencies as a result of the development and implementation of technologies. The statistics show, that intra-company international transfer of technologies of North American

TNCs accounts for 44.2% of world exports of OIP (World Development Indicators report, 2014).

At the same time, there is a market technological exchange between independent entities of the world economy, which is sold through the sale of OIP. Thus, the volume of foreign exchange receipts from the export of OIP of various US organizations is about 37% of the total volume (Table 5).

Table 5. The volume of foreign exchange earnings from the export of US OIP in the world, billion US dollars

Year	Total	Outside earnings	Inside earnings		
			total	Head quarters in the USA from foreign branches and subsidiaries	subsidiaries and affiliates of the United States from foreign companies
2011	108,3	40,1	68,2	64,8	3,4
2010	105,6	39,2	66,4	63,1	3,3
2006	70,7	20,3	50,4	46,9	3,5
1998	35,6	9,3	26,3	24,4	2,0
1994	26,7	6,4	20,3	19,3	1,0
1990	16,6	3,4	13,3	12,9	0,4
1986	8,1	1,9	6,2	6,0	0,2

Source: World receipts of royalties and license fees by region, 2009 and 2010//World Trade Organization [Electronic resource]. - 2011. - Mode of access: http://www.wto.org/english/res_e/statis_e/its2011_e/its11_trade_category_e.htm. - Date of access: 01.04.2017.

The international transfer of technologies is manifested not only in the sale of scientific and technical results, but also in their transfer through the conclusion of a cross-licensing and/or cross-licensing agreement that primarily aims at achieving strategic goals, rather than making a profit.

Implementation of international technology transfer within the corporate network and between independent companies takes place through direct and indirect transfer channels. The classical direct channel for technology transfer is foreign direct investment (FDI), and the indirect channel refers to the diffusion of technologies in different forms of manifestation for host countries.

Nowadays the role of direct technology transfer is growing through the conclusion of contractual relations between independent business partners (unrelated to each other's participation in capital). This manifests itself in such non-joint forms of organization of international business as contract manufacturing, licensed production, franchising, outsourcing services, contract management. Transfer of technology through contractual relations, not related to equity participation, allows recipient countries to integrate into the global production chains of more powerful companies in the donor country. If the volumes of FDI attracted to the country are insignificant, then non-joint forms of cooperation are extremely relevant. These forms are the international incentives for international companies to invest in maintaining the viability of their partners in the dissemination of knowledge, technology and skills.

Subsequently, the direct transfer channel will facilitate the diffusion of technologies and provide a stimulating indirect effect on mutually beneficial cooperation between firms and countries in different fields:

- in the exchange of information on existing technologies between companies of different countries;
- in the interaction of labor resources, possessing production, management experience and knowledge of technology adaptation within the framework of affiliated and independent companies of several countries;
- in the interrelationships between TNCs and independent companies of the donor country with local suppliers of goods and services of the recipient country in order to transfer experience and knowledge on the organization of an effective system of supply of goods and services, quality management and company management, adaptation of technologies to local conditions.

Thus, through the direct and indirect channels of technology transfer between interacting entities in the world economy, three types of economic relations are formed.

The first group of intra-firm organizational-economic relations arises about the transfer of technology by an international company and a foreign structure created by foreign direct investment (a branch, joint venture or subsidiary) through the use of commercial and non-commercial forms of transfer.

The second includes contractual commercial relations between two independent firms of different countries that are not connected by participation in each other's capital and which are manifested in non-joint forms of international business: licensing agreements and contracts for contract manufacturing, outsourcing services, franchising, and management contracts.

The third group of purely market relations involves the conclusion of contracts between independent entities, the subject of which is the purchase and sale of technology.

The nature of economic relations regarding the international transfer of technology depends, first of all, on the motives of the actors participating in it, which at the micro level are determined by their individual, specific characteristics (for example, the presence of redundant technologies, the stage of the life cycle, the lack of resources for independent use of technology, the need for a cross licensing, the procedure for determining the cost and pricing of technology, etc.). In addition to micro level reasons, the motivations of companies for international technology transfer may be influenced by factors of meso- and macro levels: technological dynamics and intensity of market competition in the industry, the presence of cross-cultural similarities/differences between firms, their geographical proximity or remoteness, and the magnitude of the technological gap between firms and countries.

From the perspective of the life cycle and economic benefits for the subjects of technology transfer, they can be classified into three groups.

1. Technology of the first level, creating a new, including a foreign market, which allows obtaining a monopolistically high profit to its owner. This is possible due to the fact that the target market is not yet saturated with goods produced with the help of this technology.

First of all, there are no local competitive firms capable of producing similar products due to the presence of large technological barriers to entry into a particular industry market.

2. As a result of the development of globalization processes, the deepening of the international division of labor and the saturation of the market with goods, technology that has created a new market is shifting to the level of technology that allows expansion to other target markets. In this case, technology makes it possible to form a market niche. Technology of the second level does not allow its owner to obtain a monopoly profit. However, it gives an opportunity to enter the industry market, where in the competitive process an average price level is established, which allows the company to profit and maintain its position in the industry market.
3. The further increase in knowledge and the development of scientific and technological progress objectively leads to physical and moral wear and tear of technology, as a result of which it passes to the final stage of the life cycle and becomes a technology contributing to the improvement of the structure of the value of the goods. This technology does not allow you to achieve a monopolistically high profit or to win additional sales markets. It provides an opportunity to stay on the industry market by reducing the material consumption, energy intensity, labor intensity of the products. However, this technology of the third level can and really prolongs the period of its existence at the expense of foreign markets.

Consequently, the most important motives as a combination of different incentives for companies to international transfer of technology are realized in their technological strategies. In the world economy, first the American and then the Japanese technology strategy was formed, the experience of which is borrowed by firms from different countries.

When the global enterprise creates innovations, the added value is the sum of the compounded costs associated with the development of the intellectual property object and its legal protection.

These costs are calculated for the entire duration of the innovation cycle. Added value can also arise as a result of the company's acquisition of intellectual property rights for innovations (new technologies, design documentation for new products) created by other enterprises. Using of these innovations results in additional inflows of money (Wong G, et al., 2010, 386-398).

In this case, the added value is the sum of the discounted cash flows generated as a result of applying or transferring innovation in the production activity of the enterprise. Formation of the added value of material and intellectual assets as a result of the creation or acquisition of innovation leads to increasing market value, which is a strategic direction of the enterprise development nowadays.

Transfer of technologies includes a whole list of elements related to different types of innovation. This could be the transfer of patents to inventions, patent licensing, transfer of technological documentation, trade non-patent inventions, transfer of "know-how", information exchange with personal communication (seminars, conferences, exhibitions, symposiums, etc.), transfer of technological information accompanying the acquisition or lease (leasing) of technological equipment and machines, scientific research and development in the exchange of scientists and experts, the organization of joint production or enterprise, etc. (Table 6).

It should be noted that participants in the innovation process face a number of institutional and market problems. For example, developers, intermediaries, owners of new technologies often face difficulties in finding users and buyers of new products or technologies or partners to create or develop productions

Also, the developers themselves (researchers, scientists) do not have sufficient skills to promote goods/technology to the market, doing business. Some of global corporations have difficulties in obtaining the necessary information. Namely: if the company plans achieve competitive advantages by improving the technology of their work, then inevitably raises the question of where to find information about technologies that can improve business performance.

Table 6 Types of innovations' transferring

#	Classification feature	Type of transferring	Definition
1	Contract type	Direct	The involved parties find each other themselves
		Classic	Transfer between participants takes place on the basis of established relationships (for example, state-research institute-enterprise)
		Mediated	The transfer is with the involvement of intermediary
2	Exchange level	Internal	The transfer of technology from one units of the organization to another
		Quasi-internal	Transfer between legally interrelated organizations (subsidiaries, branches)
		External	Transfer between independent developers and consumers of technology
3	Area	Local	Transfer of technology between legally interconnected units and organizations
		Regional	Transfer between participants innovation process within one region
		Inter - regional	Transfer between participants from different regions of one state
		Domestic	Transfer, all participants of which are organizations of domestic market
		International	Transfer between organizations, not legally connected with each other, functioning in the territories of different countries
4	Technology type	Substitute	All or most of the properties system, in connection with which the new technology replaces the previous one
		Rationalizing	Change in quantitative or qualitative properties of the system, rearrangement of the components of the system to improve its functioning
		Expanding	The qualitative change in the original properties of the system, the original concept without changing the functional principle
		Opening	Qualitative change of initial properties of the system, the original concept with a change in the functional principle

Source: author's survey.

To address these problems, the activities of various organizations are directed, acting as intermediaries in the market of innovative products. These are centers transfer/transfer of technology, scientific and educational centers, business innovation centers, etc. At the heart of their functioning lies the assistance to participants in innovative processes in the implementation of their innovative capabilities and potential.

The complexity of the relationship between the participants of the innovation process provides opportunities for the application of a variety of forms and methods how to transfer technology. For their disclosure, we consider the main stages of technological transfer taking into account its key participants (Table 7).

From an economic point of view, technology transfer takes two forms. It can be both commercial and non-commercial.

The transfer of non-commercial technologies is most often development and application of fundamental scientific research. Concerning commercial transfer, it is based on economic relations, with the help of which the innovation developed in one organization becomes a commercial product/process used by another organization. These relations are quite complex characters and are distinguished by the following features:

- the desire of the developer to gain competitive advantages due to the technology, and therefore, to protect it as an object of intellectual property, including special terms of contracts;
- incomplete alienability of the technology from its developer;
- needs for the transfer of implicit knowledge, which requires the training of the host parties;
- active participation of the developer in the process of technology transfer.

Thus, in Germany, the functions of technological intermediaries between the scientific-research centers and enterprises are carried out by various scientific societies and joint research associations in industry.

Table 7. Methods of innovations' transferring

#	Classification feature	Method of transferring	Definition
1	The nature of the promotion technology in the process of its transferring	Horizontal	The subject of the transfer is itself technology
		Vertical	Products are manufactured on the basis of new technology
2	Number of participants	Direct	Technology is transferred directly from developer to the consumer
		Indirect	Technology is transferred with the participation of intermediaries who are not developers, or consumers
3	Market	Domestic	Technology is transmitted internally
		International	International technology transfer
4	Process	Completed	Both sides (transmitting and receiving) invite the intermediaries for getting opportunities in technology transfer and facilitate the transfer process
		Not completed	The transferring party is not obligatory for a technology developer, and the receiving party may not use it for production of products

Source: author's survey.

For example, the Fraunhofer Society, which performs the leading organizational role in this interaction, includes 58 research institutes, whose activities are funded by both federal government subsidies and income from implementation of studies on a contract basis.

Most universities in developed countries have structural departments responsible for the university's interaction with enterprises. Some countries (for example, Finland and the USA) notice the technology transfer as a formal function; it is enshrined in the status of the third mission of universities (in addition to educational and scientific-research). At the same time, we note that the improper performance of this function entails depriving the University of the Rights to the intellectual own (Weinstein N, et al., 2008, 456-476).

4.3. Innovative Entrepreneurship in Global Environment

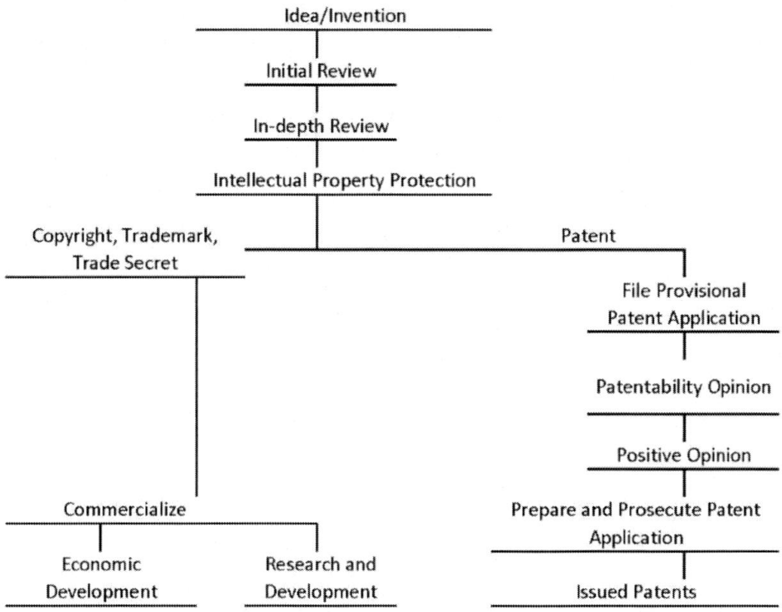

Source: Author's survey.

Figure 4. Transfer and commercialization of innovations.

Commercialization of developments is aimed at obtaining a commercial result and begins with the discovery of the prospects for commercial use of the new development, and ends with the implementation of the development (technology, obtained with its help of the product or service provided) in the market and obtaining a commercial effect (Figure 4).

The process of commercialization of scientific and technical developments, as well as physical, biological and any other processes in nature, society and science, has various parameters at the input (it starts with an idea, a model, a small series) and is multicomponent (includes a different number of stages, different partners, various resources, etc.).

Accordingly, the results at the output (the result of commercialization may be the sale of a license, the conclusion of a contract for further work, co-production, etc.) will be also different.

Scientific activity is a specific branch of the global economy, developing according to its international and domestic laws. The nature of scientific research in various branches of science and technology dictates its own characteristics, its stages of work. Each stage of research and development work is completed by obtaining a specific result that has a certain commercial value.

However, these results can have a variety of forms. These can be reports on scientific discoveries, experimental and experimental samples of new instruments and installations, new technological processes, as well as new products of high degree of readiness and much more.

Accordingly, the commercialization of these results can take various forms and features, depending on the particular stage of research and development. The results of research and development work in the market should meet all the requirements for the product as an element of the market mechanism, but they have a number of features.

Among the general characteristics for any product, the product in the technology market has significant features, primarily related to the specifics of scientific and technical development as an object of intellectual property. Secondly, the commercial result still lays a long way from scientific and technical development to obtaining its buyer in a specific market. And, at last, the innovation has to bring the novelty to the market.

Among the most important specific characteristics of scientific and technological development as a commodity, we can distinguish the following:

- owner of intellectual property,
- the value of intellectual property,
- state of development (prototype, layout, etc.).

Of particular importance are characteristics common to all types of goods, such as operating conditions, safety and environmental friendliness, competitive advantages and results of comparative tests, engineering services for implementation and operation, and the ability to adapt to the requirements of a particular customer.

It should be noted that the new technology, like any other product, should have a host (owner of intellectual property) and a price (have an estimate of the value of intellectual property).

When solving the problem of entering the world market of technologies, it is necessary to think about the interests and behavior of buyers in this market. The buyer in the industrial market makes a decision based on a detailed review and assessment of available technological alternatives in order to choose the most appropriate option for a particular project or investment strategy taking into account the socio-economic and environmental conditions.

The choice of a suitable development is directly related to the conditions of its use in specific situations. One of the most important factors in the choice of developments, especially for developing countries, is the possibility of competitive production for the target markets.

Accounting for all of these factors leads to the real commodity in the technology market is not the development itself, but a whole technological package that includes, in addition to the actual development, a number of additional elements.

First of all, they pay attention to the degree of development of the so-called engineering services, involving technical assistance in the introduction of the development and operation of equipment, assistance to industrial firms in reducing their costs for maintenance and repair of new equipment.

An important element of the technology package is the ability to adapt the development to the features of its use by a specific consumer, adaptation to local conditions.

High potential commercialization has specific developments, technologies, as well as technical, organizational and other solutions, especially in case of transfer from one industry and application area to others (Teece D., 1986. 78).

The best examples of innovations' customization belong to American and Japanese companies, so let's discuss their strategies of innovation's transferring.

According to the Japanese strategy, the transfer of patented unique OIP to highly specialized industries is carried out in developed countries, and in developing countries we can see the transfer of standardized OIP to traditional industries.

The transfer of standardized, obsolete OIP occurred mainly in the countries of South-East Asia, which have the least technological gap with Japan, through FDI in the creation of joint ventures. C. McMillan confirms that there was a transfer of OIP, which are at the last stages of the life cycle: "... the capital abroad was invested in industries that are experiencing a decline in Japan itself", and in the Japanese market development of advanced industries and "... exports of industries on the rise" (Tavares A., 2016, 76-78). The main task in this case is the transfer of organizational, managerial experience and knowledge based on the achieved level of scientific and technological development. At the same time, technology transfer through training and transfer of experience promote diffusion and transfer of technologies to the territory of the recipient country (Sutton J., 1997, 99).

The presence of a minimum technological gap in the international transfer of technology in the domestic market of the recipient country leads to cooperation of donor companies with local firms, to increase labor productivity, to produce modified, improved products and to gradually increase the quality of human and scientific and technical potentials of the recipient entity. Practice confirms that the labor productivity of companies with foreign capital is several times higher than the efficiency of local producers. They are more active in R&D and achieve higher growth in wages and labor productivity, which is due to the use of foreign technologies. It is noteworthy that in developing and transition countries, labor productivity growth was observed in industries whose companies actively interacted with companies of industries with a foreign share of ownership, which indicates the existence of cooperative ties between them.

And as firms that have a foreign share of ownership, TNC's affiliated structures often act.

The most attractive countries in the international transfer of Japanese technology packages are the developing countries of the Asian region, Western and Eastern Europe, and South America.

The rate of growth in foreign exchange earnings from exports of Japanese trademarks for the period from 2005 to 2010 in China was 25%, in Taiwan 15%, Thailand 14%, while in the USA 6%, and in the world volume 9% (Royalties and license fees, 1986-2011). Thus, Japan's FDI in 2011 was mainly directed to OECD countries (56% of total FDI).

However, the growth rate of FDI inflows for the period 2004-2011 amounted to 212% for this region, and for Asian countries - 325%. The share of the countries of the Asian region accounted for about 35% of Japanese FDI in 2011. The most attractive markets were Malaysia, China, Singapore, Philippines. In addition to these countries and OECD countries, recipients of Japanese FDI were the countries of South America, including Chile and South Africa.

FDI contributes to the formation of affiliated structures and the transfer of technology. Thus, the largest share of Japan's affiliated structures falls on Asian countries that are not part of the OECD - 54%, developing countries in Western and Eastern Europe (2%) and Latin America (5%). Unfortunately, the data of international statistics do not contain information on the value of intra-company exports and imports of goods, services and OIP. The total volume of imports of affiliated structures of developing Asian countries was 38%, and exports - 49%, developing countries of Western and Eastern Europe - 1.7% and 1.9% respectively (Mendel P, et al., 2008). The given statistical data confirm that the subjects of the donor country in the case of implementing the Japanese technology strategy are geographically close to countries with cross-cultural similarities.

The North American technological strategy of international technology transfer is radically different from the Japanese one. The strategy of the United States of America, domestic and foreign authors define as profit-oriented. Its implementation is carried out by creating affiliated structures and independent companies in the territory of the host country to obtain full control over its assets, including intangible ones, located abroad with the application of an individual and absorbing market strategy (Mansfield E., 1986, 67). And the transfer of technology can be carried out in countries where there is a large technological gap. According to foreign scientists, if the technological gap between the North American donor company and the company of the recipient country exceeds 10 years, there is a transfer of "... already obsolete products and newly developed ones; modern equipment is supplied; technical documentation for new technological processes is transferred; confidential commercial information is disclosed; it is possible to use the marketing network of the technology supplier; the experience of international management is transmitted". The basis of this strategy is the transfer of a new OIP, which is patentable to the host country, which can be patented on the territory of the recipient country to win a monopoly on its use and protect its competitive advantages.

High patent activity of non-residents on the territory of developing countries of Asian, Latin American and African regions can be justified by this circumstance: Philippines (95.1%), Mexico (93.5%), Singapore (90.8%), Brazil (88.1%), South Africa (87.8%), Chile (80%), and India (78.8%). These countries do not belong to the main consumers of North American OIP. However, at the beginning of the XXI century the market of these countries became attractive to the United States during the international transfer of OIP (Nicholas T., 2011, 45).

The largest growth rate of foreign exchange earnings from the exports of North American OIP for the period from 2005 to 2010 is observed in Brazil (29%), India (25%), Taiwan (25%), China (23%), Argentina (21%), South Africa (13%), and the Republic of Korea (12%) (Sang Ch., 2014, 56-87). It should be noted that the international transfer of technology by the United States to Asian countries (in particular India, Malaysia, Singapore, Taiwan), Latin American (Brazil) and European (Ireland) region is carried out on the basis of the contract "982", supplying 98% of all necessary elements within two days after the conclusion of the contract (Nicholas T., 2011, 45).

At the beginning of the XXI century the most attractive region for the transfer of USA technologies has become developing countries and countries with economies in transition. The growth rate of North American FDI in these countries over the period from 2004 to 2010 amounted to 141%, while for OECD countries only 30%. In turn, developing countries in the Asian region in terms of inflows of FDI to the United States achieved a growth rate of about 279% over the same period.

A promising area for the international transfer of North American technologies is their transfer to the countries of South America, in particular in Chile. In 2010, this country received US$ 4.5 billion of North American FDI, which corresponds to the level of developed countries, such as Germany ($ 3.2 billion) and Japan ($ 6.4 billion). Among the countries of the African region can be identified South Africa, which actively attracts the United States OIP and reached the growth rate of US FDI for the period of 2010-2014 years at 59% (Rassenfosse G., 2012, 45).

Thus, the international transfer of technology in developing countries and countries with economies in transition mainly takes place according to the strategy of the parent company, whose affiliated structures are located on their territory. Unlike developed countries, about 58% of affiliated structures of TNCs are based on the territory of these States.

Nowadays the market of high-tech services and contract manufacturing is widely spread in developing countries (Brazil, India, China, Malaysia, Taiwan, and Singapore) and countries with transitional economies (Belarus, Russia, Ukraine, etc.). In developing and transition economies, about 16 million employees (or 80% of the total) are employed in international contract manufacturing, outsourcing of services, franchising, licensing, management contracts, in some countries they provide about 15% of GDP. Developing countries account for about 80% of the world's exports from these activities. In 2011, among the top ten global outsourcing companies in the Global Services 100 ranking, only two were from the US, the rest from Asia (India, China, Philippines) and countries with transitional economies (Russia). For example, Belarusian companies as EPAM Systems, IBA Group, iTransition and Intetics are also included in the list of 100 Global Services.

Thus, the strategy of international technology transfer and developing countries with transitional economies can be defined as aimed at the development of contractual relationships not related to equity participation, mainly represented by transactions on cross-border contract manufacturing and service outsourcing. The strategy of the countries is realized by transfer of technologies to the states with cross-cultural similarities and differences due to the implementation of offensive and individual competitive strategies using the principles of market pricing in order to include companies of countries in the global value chains of foreign organizations.

Management of enterprises in the high-tech sector of the economy must take into account the innovative component of the strategy when formulating a strategy for sustainable development. This component covers creation of innovations, acquisition or their attraction on the basis of license agreements. Strengthening the innovative component of the company's strategy involves the development or availability of an economically and financially sound plan of action. This plan may include the independent creation by the enterprise of innovations or acquisition of other objects of intellectual property from other enterprises, based on innovative developments. When choosing one of these areas, it is necessary to have a method of economic justification for one or another direction of strengthening the innovative component of the company's competitive strategy.

Geographically Dispersed Team (GDT) is a group of people working together from different parts of the country or the world over a single project. Members of the virtual team communicate only through electronic technology and meet each other on-line. Virtual teams allow companies to hire the most talented professionals, while not bringing them inconvenience and not changing their place of residence.

Let’s consider the main types of virtual teams that currently exist in companies. Depending on the time zone, goals and roles of members, virtual teams can be divided into 8 categories:

1. Network Team. Traditionally members of such a team are at a great distance from each other. It differs in that such virtual teams include “temporary” members who, after performing certain tasks, are

excluded from this team. The life cycle of the team lasts until all the goals are achieved. Widely used in consulting and IT companies;

2. Parallel Teams. Usually they are formed from the employees of one company. While team members fulfill their basic role in the company, they are added one more role to achieve some goal. Such a team is formed very quickly, to consider the task that has arisen and to solve it quickly. Unlike network teams, have a permanent composition of team members;
3. Virtual team for product/project development (Project or Product Development Teams). The classic type of commands, which appeared in the 90's. Specialists from different regions and points of the planet are united for joint product development;
4. Work/production/functional team (Work, Production or Functional Teams). Members of such a team are formed to perform daily tasks. The role of each member of such a team is clearly defined and everyone works independently of the other. Ultimately, the results of each team member are combined into a common;
5. Service Teams. In this case we are talking about virtual service teams that work from different parts of the world and perform the function of customer support 24/7;
6. Initiative Teams (Action Teams). Members of the initiative team come together to immediately solve current problems. Once the problem is solved - it dissolves;
7. Management Team. Formed by company managers who are in different cities and countries to discuss strategies and activities at the corporate level;
8. Offshore ISD Team. Many companies transfer part of their production to other countries, where its content is much more profitable (India, Philippines, etc.). The team that works there is called offshore.

Features of the formation of teams affect the other factors of its functioning: from the internal organization of the team to the necessary level of control by the project manager over the participants.

The interaction of geographically distributed (virtual) teams has become the norm applied everywhere, from global software development projects to research and support of business processes in companies of various industries. However, global software development projects have an ambiguous reputation.

Proponents of global software development prove that it offers a number of advantages: cost reduction, fast product release to the market, access to experienced professionals and faster updating (Popay J, et al., 2006, 88-90). Opponents and skeptics, in turn, call global development the "failure of the last decade", emphasizing that the perceived advantages are not always realized and they are mistakenly perceived as given.

Why are some global projects successful, while others fail? Let's try to answer this question.

First of all, it should be noted that projects are of different types, not all of them are distributed, and not all participate in virtual teams have the same access. There are also differences in the way the team is formed, and distributed projects could be called virtual, because the teams working on them consist of people from different regions.

But similar projects can be implemented by loosely coupled teams, consisting of several groups located in different places, in which the participants work side by side. Virtual teams are characterized by a high level of interdependence and cooperation of participants. The situation is more complicated when globalization is provided through offshore outsourcing (transfer of work under a contract to a third party) or insourcing (development by a foreign subsidiary). Depending on the specifics of the formation of teams, in particular, the level of control exercised by the project leader over participants at remote locations may depend.

Given the complexity of the very phenomenon of global software development, we will focus on global projects carried out by globally dispersed or virtual teams. A virtual team is a group of geographically, organizationally or temporally dispersed workers united through information and communication technologies to jointly solve one or more tasks. Virtual teams are different from traditional c-sharing by the fact that the participants of the first teams keep their independence when working on their tasks. A virtual team can be both a permanent structure and a temporary structure in which participants with certain skills are combined to achieve some results or fulfill specific customer requirements.

Typically, virtual teams are looked at as teams in general (from the point of view of sociology) or teams in the context of information systems, consisting of marketing specialists, users and project owners, managers responsible for drafting requirements, maintenance specialists and software developers. In 2004, the research group Ann Powell published an exhaustive survey of the status of virtual teams based on information systems. The authors note that studies usually do not identify the types of projects suitable for virtual teams; the optimum number and range of skills of participants in virtual teams dealing with projects of various types is not established; do not specify the typical characteristics of virtual teams and the optimal structure of teams (self-organizing and managed), as well as the role of leadership. Moreover, it is noted that more than 90% of research publications were based on student projects, which are known to be carried out in controlled environments. Ten years later, all these issues remained relevant, especially in relation to virtual software development teams.

Many years of experience in managing software development projects, as well as in design and research projects, showed that, despite the many advantages of modern communications and interaction, the effectiveness and effectiveness of virtual teams still strongly depend on mutual trust and team spirit, especially in global environment. In virtual teams, you need to communicate with colleagues from other offices as closely as with employees near you. Therefore, we should not underestimate the importance of supporting unanimity and the desire to jointly achieve a common goal. All the successes of a virtual team are worth noting together, regardless of who mastered the first, who came up with the original idea or who had the biggest load.

At the same time, it is important that each office has a responsibility for some strictly defined directions, modules or products, so that it would be proud and there was no sense of separation from the center. Perhaps this sound like a contradiction - unanimity is required, but everyone should have their own duties, so some balance is needed.

The main task in forming a virtual team is to select participants and distribute assignments in such a way that the competencies of the staff mutually complement each other. With regard to management, it is important to monitor the effectiveness of the virtual team and to identify interference at an early stage. The head of the virtual team can achieve the necessary level of transparency by controlling key performance indicators.

Virtual teams form dense networks, in which it is easier to create a transparent hierarchical order of problem solving in comparison with loosely coupled ones. In addition, virtual teams have more advantages in terms of the ability to interact with customers, especially if they also have many representative offices in different regions. For such a network to be efficient, regular meetings and long trips to other offices are needed to establish closer relations. This will help to differentiate the basic skills; mentality and culture from the risks for the project into opportunities for its development (Table 8).

Virtual teams bring tangible benefits to the business. Firstly, it is economy. The company can avoid the huge costs of real estate, office space, utilities, office equipment and stuff. In addition, the organization is able to open its representative offices in regions with low costs for business, production, etc., which will also reduce its costs.

In addition, the company does not spend its budget on travel of employees and their corporate travel to work, corporate transport, cars, and the lack of time spent on movement makes it possible to direct the resources of employees to a good cause. The lack of a geographical framework allows the company to choose any specialist from anywhere in the world, to unite experts and specialists from all over the world to work on the project.

It is difficult not to note the higher productivity of such a team, because, as a rule, virtual teams have a flatter organizational structure in comparison with a traditional team and clearly set goals for each participant, thus avoiding slow decision-making. The fast speed of achieving the result of such a command is also provided almost round the clock work on the "product", as its members are often in different time zones.

Table 8. On-line services for virtual operations

Name of service	Definition
Skype	Free access program, with which you can call friends, colleagues, wherever they are. The program allows you freely and, most importantly, to communicate for free on the Internet. Skype uses P2P technology to connect with other users to communicate on the network. Provides free calls to mobile and landline phones
GoToMeeting	This is another service created for communication. It has such opportunities as the organization of wide demonstrations, videoconferences, presentations, online meetings with colleagues and brainstorming. The developers have tried to create the most tangible and almost real connection with all participants of the session, so you can work with the team in GoToMeeting without unnecessary obstacles. It supports simultaneous communication of up to 100 participants, has many useful functions such as integration with Microsoft Outlook and other MS Office applications, etc.
Google+ hangouts	Free access service for chat, calls and group video calls. It offers a screen demonstration, joint drawing on the whiteboard, editing documents in Google Docs and conducting broadcast webinars. Available on mobile platforms
Dropbox	This is a cloud-based data warehouse that allows users to store their data on servers and share them with other users. Synchronizes folders with the server and other computers. Allows you to configure folders for collaboration or a public folder accessible to everyone. Uses Amazon's S3. 2GB - for free. There is a business version
Google Drive	Service for storing and synchronizing files, serving as a file system for other Google services. Allows you to synchronize files between your online account, computers and mobile devices. There is a version history, OCR, online search. Provides 5 GB free
Basecamp	A simple and effective project management system. Contains tasks, calendar, discussions, profiles, wiki documents, files, project log. Easily allows you to organize joint work with customers and partners. Supports mobile access
Wrike	Allows you to create tasks, group them by project and track the progress of their execution. The main advantage of the service is the more advanced functionality compared to the competitors for collaboration. Contains network schedule and project reports. Allows you to set reminders and log task time

Source: Author's survey.

Nevertheless, despite all the advantages of virtual teams, their effectiveness is questionable. For example, in 70 virtual teams there were found that 82% of them did not meet their goals, and 33% rated their cooperation as unsuccessful. Similarly, a study by Deloitte found that 66% of virtual IT teams failed to meet customer requirements (Tabak R, et al., 2012, 77).

Virtual teams can help to transfer innovations, because they provide more creative environment, interrelations without distance, so employees may share their ideas and organize discussion in effective way.

Questions for discussion (Chapter 4):

1. What is the structure of innovative corporation?
2. How does core competence is formed in competitive environment?
3. What types of transferring innovation do exist?
4. Why it is important to customize the innovations?
5. What is the role of virtual teams and structures in transferring of innovations?

Chapter 5

PLANNING AND ORGANIZATION OF INTERNATIONAL RESEARCH AND DEVELOPMENT

5.1. MODELS OF R&D PLACEMENT

Placement of R&D units is a strategic task for modern organizations. Since the geographical movement of R&D units is very difficult due to the large investments in their opening. Their placement takes into account not only the level of financial investments, but also many other conditions that have a direct impact on the development of competitive advantages of the organization in the long term. In these conditions there may be local conditions and opportunities of doing business, proximity to suppliers, the possibility of production and marketing of the final product, qualifications of involved staff, and many others.

For effective choice of location of R&D units the following models are used: technological curve, technological portfolio matrix, modified Porter's model of competition, etc.

The model of the technological curve assumes that each technology has its natural limit, and as it approaches it, increasing specific investments are required to improve the parameters of the product (process). These assumptions are reflected in the choice of an S-curve as the model. It is usually assumed to compare technologies in their performance (the possibility of achieving the best parameters of the product).

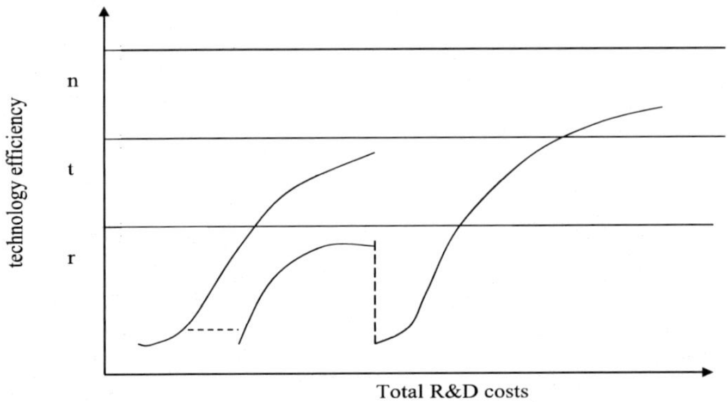

Notes:
E_n - border capabilities of the new technology
E_t - This is the boundary of possibilities of the available technology
E_r - the border of possibilities of the available technology in its development in the home country.
Source: M. Perlitz International Management. Stuttgart: Lucins & Lucins, 1997.

Figure 5. Technology curve model.

Model in Figure 5 reflects the features of the internationalization of research and development. This is an opportunity to transfer R&D abroad to achieve the same results with less investment due to the lower cost of resources abroad (point D), as well as a faster growth of efficiency and, perhaps, even raising its boundaries due to a different scientific and production culture, the influence of related technologies (point F). The transition of a large firm from

Mature technology to just nascent (B-C transition) is the most important point in technology policy. Among emerging technologies, there may be those that threaten the very existence of existing business. Usually, the performance of technologies is compared by comparing the main parameter of interest to the main consumer; the new technology is considered promising if it allows achieving the same or better performance than the old one.

There are two main problems:

1. consumers can be satisfied with lower values of the compared parameter and the new technology will be competitive in this regard.
2. the new technology can create a product with new properties or significantly improve the parameters important for other groups of consumers.

In practice, business vision was repeated many times the situation when the market leader has studied the possibilities and came to a new segment created by the nascent technology, which was considered attractive and was lost after some time as the possibility of the successful development of new niches and their positions on the traditional market.

The mechanism of "catastrophe" is that initially a new technology is not only satisfied with basic consumers, but not profitable to the manufacturers and market leaders. It does not provide sufficient volume and satisfies only the lower, poorer segments of consumers, which together leads to a slight profitability of the new technology or even its loss for a large company. Often, new technology is born within the leading firms, but rejected by them, and to catch up with independent innovators subsequently fails, despite the greater financial power, as the life cycle of high-tech products is very short (up to 2 years) and about the same period is needed to launch the product. For example, Seagate Technology (Scotts Valley) in California, USA was founded in 1980 and by the mid-80 became the leader among hard drive manufacturers.

In the mid-1970s, its turnover amounted to $700 million. The company was a pioneer in the development of the 5.25-inch drive market and held a dominant position as an IBM supplier and manufacturer of IBM-compatible personal computers. Seagate engineers second in the industry have created a working prototype of a 3.5-inch drive. At the beginning of 1985, 80 copies of the new model were collected with the help of small funding from the company. The results were presented to the company's leading marketers, and a press release was issued with a message about the active work on the 3.5-inch drive.

However, the most important buyer of Seagate products - IBM, as well as other manufacturers of personal computers such as AT, showed no interest in the new product, as it needed 40 - and 60-megabyte drives, and prototypes had a capacity of only 10 MB. As a result, Seagate marketers have lowered their sales forecasts for the new model (Scherer F., 1983 109-123).

The managers responsible for production and finance, based on market forecasts and analysis of possible costs, concluded that the new type of drive will never be competitive with 5.25-inch on such an important indicator as the price per 1 MB of memory. Accordingly, the profitability of 3.5-inch drives will be significantly lower than 5.25-inch.

Seagate needed to replace the 5.25 - inch ST 412 drive, which was at the end of its life cycle, with sales of $300 million, while the entire market for 3.5-inch drives was estimated at $50 million. Hence, the top managers of the company rationally concluded that the new type of drive is not suitable for production in terms of profitability, or in terms of gaining market share, in the production of a new 5.25-inch drive, which had a number of technological improvements. While the attention of Seagate's management was focused on the full - scale personal computer market, their former employees, frustrated by the delay in implementing their brainchild, organized a new company - Conner Peripherals.

This company focused on the release of 3.5-inch drives for the growing market of portable and small desktop PCs. The main buyer was the company Compaq Computer, which Seagate has never focused. At first, Seagate was not concerned about this turn of events. Things were going well, the new company focused on a small niche (strength, reliability, small size and weight). Stimulated by the growing market of portable computers, Conner increased the capacity of its hard drive by 50% annually. By the end of 1987, 3.5-inch drives had already met the requirements of the main market of personal computers.

When the Seagate started to react and come up with a strategy against a competitor in this market, it was too late; competition positions have already been lost.

There are supporting technologies that modify the existing production, and alternative, changing the smooth development in the direction of improving the characteristics of the final product.

Making decisions the management of the company is forced to pay attention to the following issues:

- whether the technology is supportive or alternative;
- whether alternative technology is strategically important (promising);
- what market niche will be the basis for the development of alternative technology;
- in what organizational forms alternative technology will be created and developed.

Signal to senior management of the company, speaking about what a certain technology is an alternative, is the difference in the assessment of its prospects on the intra-firm level from the different functional services: ardent supporters of a new technology often become researchers and designers, while marketers and financiers because of their specific point of view rarely enthusiastic about these innovations.

The prospect of alternative technologies is evaluated differently than supportive. In modern firms, there is a practice of supporting feedback from the main buyers, surveys which determine the technological policy of the company. Since the main buyers are usually the most demanding, their opinions stimulate the introduction of supporting technologies, but their opinion about alternative technologies can be misleading. Therefore, it is very important to ask the right questions to the main consumers. The correct question is to compare the future needs of the client and the possibilities of alternative technology, taking into account the pace of its development. Potential customers, whose needs differ from those of the main segment, can be satisfied with the new technology. These customers form the starting niche for the development of alternative technology.

One of the features of the alternative technology is a lower profitability of production on its basis at the initial stages of development (compared to supporting technologies). This fact does not allow a large Corporation to use its usual mechanisms for allocating resources and is one of the reasons why the development of alternative technology requires the creation of a separate independent organization. If the transition to an alternative technology immediately gives a good or even higher rate of return, it is painless to take root in the mother organization.

After the release of the alternative technology in the stage of maturity, it is not advisable to combine the company that stands out for its development with the parent company because of the conflicting interests and cultures of different parts of the business. History shows that such associations can lead not only to serious failures, but also to fatal crises. A large company consists of business units, each with its own life cycle. The wisdom of managers is to unlock the full potential of alternative technology, even if it kills the core business. Either the company itself closes the fading business, or it is forced to do by competitors. At the same time, in the context of globalization, it is important to search for a country in which the transition to radically new technology (especially alternative type) takes place at lower costs or is easier due to a different business or engineering culture (another way of thinking).

One of the biggest challenges in using the s-curve technology lifecycle model is determining the point at which the firm is currently located. Therefore, it is especially important to organize monitoring of the external environment and the development of the company's predictive system.

The model of the technology lifecycle helps to guide the development of the technique of "technological matrix". In Table 9 each pair of indicators "technological attractiveness-resource potential" compares a certain market and financial strategy.

The application of this model in the practice of the IOC has the peculiarity that it is necessary to take into account whether the firm adheres to the technological policy of "center-for-global" or "local-for-local", and accordingly to assess the technological attractiveness and resource potential or globally, or from the point of view of the local market.

Table 9. Technological matrix

Resource potential / Technological attractiveness	Low	Medium	High
Low	Escape[1]	Rationalization[1]	Selling of know-how[2]
Medium	Rationalization [1]	Presence of rationalization[2]	Niche strategy[3]
High	The acquisition of know-how[2]	Presence[3]	Leadership[3]

Source: Author's survey.

[1] strategy - reinvesting,

[2] selection,

[3] investing.

Gerpott's model offers the selection process of the host system R&D of multinational corporations (Panzano P, Roth D., 2006, 345). It facilitates decision-making on various issues.

The choice of policy in the technological sphere is determined in the model depending on the combination of the values of such indicators as the attractiveness of technology and the technological position of the enterprise. With the high attractiveness of the new technology, it is assumed to choose more capital - intensive projects, and at low-less investment activity. A good technological position is associated with a more aggressive policy in the international market, a greater degree of involvement of the company's resources in the global race, while a weaker one orients the company to cooperation on an international scale.

The process is two-step: first, the question of how the scientific and technical activities will be carried out and then where the R&D centers will be located.

At the first stage, the form of business organization in the field of R&D is determined by analyzing the technological position of the enterprise and the attractiveness of this technology. Combined strategies are more common in practice.

Table 10. The process of selecting locations for R&D centers

The maturity of technology	Customer orientation	
	Low	High
	Level 1. The Foundation to achieve competitive advantage	
Low	Research (real innovation)	Consumer-oriented R&D (following the technological advances demanded)
High	Development of technological process, product improvement (based on the price/quality ratio)	Modification of the product according to customer requirements
	Level 2 essential information from external sources (in relation to the enterprise)	
Low	Knowledge system of competitors, professional know-how	Knowledge, based on the first applications, to meet customer needs
High	Management experience, marketing research	Customer's needs and problems
	Level 3. Suitable locations for R&D	
Low	R&D activities in the vicinity of technology centers (technology parks, universities, etc.)	R&D activities in the vicinity of consumers adopting new technology
High	R&D activities in the vicinity of production sites	R&D activities in the vicinity of consumption sites

Source: Compiled by the author on the basis of T. J. Gerpott. Globales F&E-Management: Bausteine eines Gesamtkonzepts zur Gestaltung eines weltweiten P&E-Standortsystems/yintegriertes Technologie und Innovationsmanagement, Berlin, 1991.

The second stage is the assessment of R&D locations. The basis here is a three-level analysis of the external component-customer needs and (Table 10).

At the first level, the question of what competitive advantages are necessary is solved to increase the enterprise in a specific situation. Then the information from external sources is determined, which influences the formation of the selected competitive advantages. At the last level, the location of the research and/or design Department is selected.

The proposed method is based on a deeply rational way of thinking. There are some doubts about the strict attribution of specific actions to a particular domain (quadrant) without taking into account other circumstances. Among the latter, one can point to the existing location of the firm's units at the time of decision-making or the external limitations of globalization.

Model Pearson/Brachia/Bemera is based on M. Porter's rhombus of competition factors (Porter M., 1988, 67-78).

M. Porter's rhombus has been modified so that it is possible to assess the different possibilities of placing R&D centers:

- human resources are allocated among the factors of production, as the qualification of personnel in the field of R&D plays a crucial role;
- consumer "supporting industries" are replaced by "supporting technologies", as the value of technological infrastructure is determined not only at the enterprise level, but is significantly supported by the know-how available at scientific institutions (research institutes, universities, etc.);
- demand has value insofar as it specifies the type of directions of development of the product or focused on specific requests of customers (the "market", "demand pull"), or promoting the technology ("technology", "technology push") - as in the first case, particular importance is proximity to markets and close contact with potential customers;
- the competition factor is less important for the choice of the location of R&D centers - it has an indirect impact through changes in the level of investment activity, but does not generate specific features for the model.

Internal factors are introduced into the modified rhombus, the marketing function playing a special role in the "market" type of product development is distinguished (Figure 6).

When placing business units in different countries, completely different problem points are revealed. In particular, such placement leads to increased costs of coordination within the enterprise (increase in organizational costs due to increased costs of communication, information, negotiations, etc.) both between units in different countries and between functional services. On the other hand, for example, direct contacts with leading consumers dramatically reduce transaction costs. This applies primarily to the market type of product development (when the technological type of savings is determined by closer contacts with the scientific community (Porter M., 2003, 77).

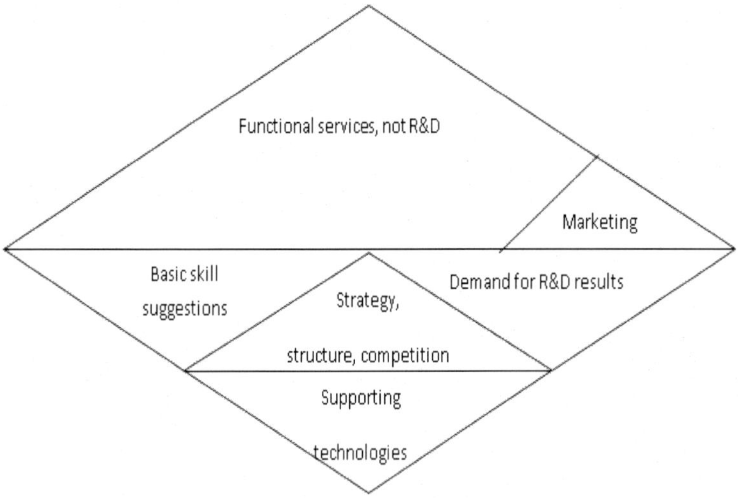

Source: M. Porter International competition. M.: International relations, 1993.

Figure 6. Modified M. porter's rhombus of competition factors.

In the 1990s, Henry Itskovits, Professor at Stanford University, developed a Triple helix model to stimulate innovation. The model describes the interaction of the academic community (Academy), business/private companies doing business (Industry), and the state to support innovation. With the expansion of influence of the company's innovative developments on society in the Triple helix model has included an additional effect of institutions: at the end of 2000-ies it was expanded by the addition of consumers (User model) and the public (Civil society). The modified model is called the Quad helix (Quadruple Helix) (Lowe R., 2001, 45-89).

In the 2010's, another spiral was added to the model - the natural environment for knowledge production - conditions for the development of innovations, new technologies across the country. This model became known as the five-part helix (Quintuple Helix).

The main goal of the innovation network for companies implementing technology policy is to create new knowledge on technology creation. Many new ideas of companies have been developed as a result of network interaction, as opposed to cases when companies create innovations in their R&D departments.

5.2. INTERNATIONAL INTEGRATION AND BUSINESS COOPERATION

The growth of the importance of innovation in the early 2000 years was confirmed by a survey conducted by Arthur D. Little, showed that 90% of the surveyed business analysts noted the growth of its importance, and 70% noted it as a key determinant in the market assessment. Such tendency determines the acceleration of the rate of passage of stages of life cycles of products and the existence of the organizations themselves. So, if before the beginning of the 19th century they were measured in centuries, in the 19th century and the first half of the 20th century - decades, in the second half of the 20th century - years and recently - months.

Scientific and technical policy, the most economically developed countries is characterized by the following:

1. the largest research projects are international, because they require so much expenditure that they require the combined efforts of different States (e.g., Hubble telescope, electronic Collider, construction and operation of space stations);
2. the development and implementation of national programs that combine the conditions of States, research centers, leading industries, contribute to the improvement of the technical level of entire industries ;

3. in addition to its own research bases, research consortia (for example, the American consortium Sematech) are created at the industry level);
4. States are increasingly exerting all kinds of pressures (from political to economic) with the aim of protecting and promoting the interests of private business representatives;
5. encouraging small and medium-sized businesses with flexibility and flexibility in implementing innovative projects (e.g., silicon valley)
6. the state creates its own centers of scientific research and forecasting of further development (for example, in Japan the Ministry of international trade and industry, publishes a 10-year "Vision"; in the United States - in the framework of the Ministry of defense operates the Agency of advanced research projects - monitor the latest scientific developments in universities, public and private laboratories and create conditions for their implementation (Pavitt K., 1982, 78).
7. the State stimulates the creative activity of employees of state laboratories, the results of which are mandatory for implementation (for example, the us Congress in the 80-90s of the XX century removed all restrictions on the commercialization of inventions obtained as a result of state grants in research centers, and provides for a system of solidarity rewards for employees of such centers - authors.

The need for the development of innovative entrepreneurship in the Russian Federation as a whole is due to global trends, but also has a number of features characteristic of domestic business:

1. global changes in the geopolitical and geo-economic structure of the modern world order;
2. increasing the intensity of the impact of factors of development of production, stimulating the application of the results of scientific and technological progress;

3. access to international markets for domestic products in connection with Russia's accession to the WTO, and at the same time facilitating access for foreign producers to the domestic market;
4. increasing the importance of scientific achievements in increasing labor productivity in modern economic entities;
5. constant growth of the level of technical armament of organizations;
6. broad information society and increasing access to mobile communications;
7. fast moral aging of the implemented equipment and technologies in the production processes.

Under the innovative entrepreneurship is proposed to understand the process of creation and commercial use of the results of scientific and technical innovations in the production activities of economic entities. Innovations may include not only changes in the products or services provided, but also in the processes of managing the activities of organizations, creating or qualitatively changing markets, developing sales channels, that is, the ability to combine new technologies, institutions and values in non-standard (previously not used) combinations.

Turning to the history of management theory, we find a lot of definitions of the concept of innovation, given in various theoretical studies, which can be classified in two main directions, which consider innovation as a result of the creative process or as a process of innovation. Currently, the pages of publications no longer find heated discussions between supporters of each of the areas that were previously. This is due to the formation of an international standard that uses innovation as a management category. Its formation was influenced by the Frascati Leadership, adopted in 1963 in the Italian city of Frascati, which provides recommendations for the collection, processing and analysis of information on science and innovation. Experts from the Organization for economic cooperation and development (OECD) are constantly monitoring the improvements and adjustments to the Guidelines. The second document adopted in 1992 is the Oslo Manual, which is a methodology for collecting data on technological innovation, thus contributing to a common approach to the concept of innovation.

Thus, innovation is the result of creative activity, for the purpose of practical use, aimed at meeting the needs of consumers.

The main features of the classification of innovations are: the degree of novelty (on it there are basic and improving), the nature of practice (management and production), the technological parameter (product and process). Let's consider each of the presented types in more detail.

Basic innovation-is aimed at the development of fundamentally new products, technologies of new generations, based on a major scientific discovery or invention. As a rule, basic innovation leads to a simultaneous breakthrough in several areas. Improving innovation-is to improve the available resources, technologies used, product improvement. Research suggests that industry leaders are keen to engage in improving innovation, while industry outsiders are more prone to basic innovation. In addition, the degree of novelty of innovation depends on the stage of the life cycle of the industry in which the organization operates, and its own. The oldest level of the industry and organization and the greatest level of the propensity to use improving technologies lead to the higher level of the likelihood of developing basic innovations.

In a managerial innovation, there have been changes in management of the entity - the use of new and improved methods of work organization structuring of tasks, distribution of involvement, and combining production resources, the use of the system of motivation, etc. Manufacturing innovations are being implemented in qualitatively new products (products), services, and the implementation of results of R&D (research and development).

It should be noted that innovation processes in many companies are too difficult, because the management systems of many companies not only do not contribute, but replace innovation processes or even block out, and sometimes completely kill innovation. It's not anyone's fault. This is simply the result of the fact that many companies are still applying management techniques that were developed forty, sixty or even a hundred years ago, management tools that were designed not for innovation and change, but for routine operations. Existing management systems and methods slow block or kill innovation. This often happens even when managers genuinely want their companies to develop and implement innovations. "But the methods they use to run their companies slow down or block innovation instead of encouraging it", - says J. Christian (Williams C. et al., 2009, 90). As a result, the so - called "organizational lag" - the delay of management innovation at a higher level of implementation of production, as a result, the effectiveness of all activities of the organization suffers.

As W. Buffett wrote in his book, "the difficulty is not to accept new ideas, but to discard old ones" (Williams C. et al., 2009, 96).

Product innovation manifests the desire to meet a certain need in the market. In the management process, production and other processes introduced new elements. When implementing innovations in terms of technological parameters is determined by the dominant design, which includes three main areas: technological design (spatial and temporal characteristics of the location of the elements), technical design (determines the ability of the end user to manage-guide innovation) and aesthetic design (image of the product or products that stimulates the consumer to purchase it).

The basis of innovative entrepreneurship is not just the transfer of technology between different industries, spheres of activity and organizations, but an adequate organization of the process of scanning and monitoring technologies, selection and analysis of information on external research and development. An effective tool in this case is a technology audit, which includes not only a review of technologies and their assessment, benchmarking, making a portfolio of own technologies of the organization, as well as the protection of innovation and its own dominant design as an object of intellectual property.

Modern business activity is characterized by a high level of requirements to the staff of organizations in the field of development and application of modern technologies, as is commonly called "creativity in the workplace". Under the creative activity is understood to be human activity, generating something qualitatively new and different uniqueness, originality and socio-historical uniqueness. Creativity is specific for a person, as it always implies the Creator-the subject of creative activity.

To understand the categories presented, it is recommended to refer to the etymology of the concept of "intellectual activity", which is based on two components - intelligence and activity. Under "intelligence" (derived from the Latin "intellectus") people understand knowledge, understanding, reason, the ability to think, rational knowledge. At the same time, if we analyze each of the components, then by "intelligence" we mean the ability to "acquire knowledge, to comprehend the laws of the objective world (knowledge); to comprehend, to comprehend the content, meaning, meaning of something (understanding); mental activity (reason), the process of reflection of objective reality in the views, judgments, concepts (the ability to think)" (Weinstein N., 2008, 88).

"Activity "means" a specific human form of attitude towards the surrounding world, the content of which is its expedient change in the interests of people. The activity includes the goal, the means, the result and the process itself".

The problems of commercialization of intellectual property in economic theory have been dealt with, in comparison with legal, relatively recently. The first studies on the impact of patent law on economic activity appeared only in the 1950s.

Notable pioneers in this area were: the British economist Edith Penrose, who conducted research in the field of mandatory patenting of inventions in those countries where they are registered and the impact of the patent system on the economic condition of developing countries, and F. Mclap, who at the request of the us Congress conducted an assessment of the economic impact of patent law.

Research in this direction was continued in the 1960s with the development of K. Arrow's concept of "insufficient ownership" of information, which were classified as promising scientific directions of intellectual property development, which were further developed in the works of such researchers as:

- economic analysis of patenting from the perspective of its impact on business (F. Sherer et al.). Research in this area has been based on the development of microeconomic models and tools, and the best patent duration, the impact of a given volume of parameters of patent formulas and the impact of compulsory licensing on the General welfare have been the basic criteria. The research of this direction was carried out within the framework of the "theory of production organization" intensively developed within the USA and EU States" (Teece D., 1986, 44);

- assessment of the impact of intellectual property rights on technological innovation and the means of their dissemination, the initiator of large-scale research in this area was E. Mansfield;
- analysis of the impact of intellectual property rights on various aspects of the economy (trade, technology transfer, foreign direct investment, etc.). It has been evolved by C. Frischtack, E. Mansfield, C. Correa (1994);
- analysis of the impact of intellectual property rights in specific sectors: information (A. Mody, 1989); semiconductors (Levin and others, 1987); the pharmaceutical industry (Taylor, C. and Z. Silberston, 1973); agriculture, including the question of the results of the protection of plant varieties through breeders' rights and patent law (see in particular: the Ministry of foreign Affairs of the Netherlands, 1990) and others;
- interdisciplinary research, including assessment of management technologies in organizations of different ownership forms, as well as non-profit organizations;
- quantification of the economic contribution of intellectual property in the form of a percentage of gross national product (GNP) and in respect of enterprises owning certain assets, including intellectual property rights.

The aim of the possession of intellectual activity and property rights is the desire of entrepreneurs to protect their own interests both in the international market and in the local and national markets, where their products are represented, including by creating all possible barriers for competitors to enter the existing markets. The recognition of the company or its products, works and services, consumer preferences to take familiar goods, the use of legislative and restrictive barriers can also act as barriers. Consider each of the barriers by example:

1. Production of fashionable clothes, when customers choose not only the style but also the brand name of the famous Couturier-Lauren Klein, J. Armani, Pierre Cardin, Alexander McQueen.

For the purchase of seven brands of alcoholic beverages, American Brands Incorporation paid the company Seagram $371.2 million. The Black Hawk trademark was sold in 1985 as part of the property of Rath Company in bankruptcy for $3 million.

2. The company "Nutra Sweet Corporation" had as its main assets patents for artificial sweetener. During the entire period of these patents, the company held a monopoly position in the market of artificial sweeteners and the income from their use reached ~ $ 1 billion per year. After the expiration of the patents in 1992, there was a 30% decrease in the cost of finished products. At the same time, in order to maintain its own position in the market, the organization was forced to expand investments in the strengthening of brands and brand names, spending up to $ 20 million per year.

In General, the study of the peculiarities of using the results of intellectual activity shows that the number of patents per capita in Spain - 10 times more than in Russia, in South Korea - 60 times more than in Russia, in Germany - 100 times more than in Russia.

On average, over the past three years 376 thousand patent applications have been filed in the US, 290 thousand in Germany and France, 190 thousand in South Korea, and only 29 thousand in Russia.

Budget revenues from the sale of science-intensive products: us $700 billion; Germany - $530 billion; Japan - $400 billion; Russia - $7 billion, which is 0.3% of the production of science-intensive products in the world.

The share of innovation-active enterprises and companies in all sectors of the economy: Russia - 9-11%, while the economically more developed countries have a share of 50% or more.

The most comprehensive definition of "intellectual property" was first given by the World Intellectual Property Organization (hereinafter WIPO), it means "the creation of the human mind: inventions, literary and artistic works, symbols, names, images, and designs used in Commerce. Intellectual property is divided into two categories:

1. industrial property that includes inventions (patents), trademarks, designs and geographical indications of origin;
2. and copyright, which includes literary and artistic works such as novels, poems and plays, films, musical works; and works of fine arts such as drawings, paintings, photographs and sculptures, as well as architectural structures. Related rights include those of performing artists, producers of phonograms in their recordings, and those of broadcasting organizations in their radio and television programmers.

The existing system of legal protection of the results of intellectual creativity began to take shape relatively recently. Only with the adoption in England in 1623 of the first law on the protection of inventor's eve 1710, the so-called Statute of Queen Anne was the beginning of the creation of such a mechanism of legal protection of works of art. The modern system of legal protection of the results of intellectual activity is multifaceted, but at the same time to strive for the unification of its norms in international law enforcement, for example, the 1948 universal Declaration of Human Rights in art. 27 declares that "everyone has the right to the protection of his moral and material interests resulting from scientific, literary or artistic works of which he is the author". This provision is further defined in article 15 of the International Covenant on economic, social and cultural rights 1966 Example of standardization is adopted in the 1883 Paris Convention for thc protection of industrial property and in 1886 - The Berne Convention for the protection of literary and artistic works and other conventions, which are discussed below, to which the Russian Federation is a party.

The main purpose of the establishment of the European communities was the need to create a single inter-communitarian economic space, built on the principles of free movement of goods, services, capital, labor, restrictions of monopolistic activity and unfair competition, which is proclaimed in the constituent documents of the European communities and reaffirmed In the Treaty on the European Union in 1992, as well as in the Treaty establishing the Constitution for Europe in 2004.

Intellectual property law, being by its nature a territorially limited right existing within only one particular state, has come into conflict with the goals and objectives facing the European communities - the creation of a fully functioning single intra-unitary economic market. The way out of this situation, despite its complexity and unwillingness of the EU member States to sacrifice at least part of their law-making powers in the field of legal protection of intellectual property, was found in the expansion of the “territorial limitation” of intellectual property rights from the territory of one particular EU member state to the scale of the entire European Union. This has been expressed, for example, in the principle of “communal exhaustion of intellectual property rights”, according to which, the owner of the protected intellectual property at the time of the first initiation of the object belonging to him in the commercial (economic) turnover through the sale anywhere in the EU loses its right to control over the further spread of the said result of intellectual property within the European Union. Thus, the protected intellectual property object freely circulates within the EU without any restrictions.

A significant factor that led to the beginning of the processes of unification and harmonization of intellectual property rights in the European Union, was the activities of the Court of justice of the EU, which in its decisions on a number of cases related to the existence and implementation of intellectual property rights within the European communities brought the intellectual property right out of domestic regulation into the orbit of the communitarian order, using the elements in its competence and the binding decisions of the court of the EU. In this regard, the decision of the EU court of Justice against Microsoft, when the court recognized the concept of "necessary infrastructure" developed in the US as a way of limiting the possibility of a dominant enterprise to develop other organizations and bring similar and innovative products and services to the market, and defined it as an "abuse" of its exclusive rights. As a result of the decision, the European Commission received additional rights to control monopolies and organizations with a dominant position, through the possession of exclusive rights.

Thus, the court of justice of the EU not only protects the exclusive rights of the right holders, but also prevents all possible distortions that may adversely affect the innovative development and competition in connection with the use and protection of economic entities of their interests. In Der Grüne Punkt, for example, the EU court of Justice held that the existence of an enterprise's exclusive rights to a trademark was not an excuse for competition infringement. Der Grüne Punkt, using its exclusive rights, forced its customers to put their own logo on the packaging of goods produced by them (even if they were made by other organizations), and the royalties were calculated based on the total number of packages produced. As a result, contacting competitors was not cost-effective for customers.

A significant role in the processes of unification and harmonization of intellectual property rights in the European Union is played by the activities of the European Commission, which has identified specific areas, mechanisms and ways of legal protection of intellectual property in the EU. The above is connected with the adoption of a number of documents by the European Commission, which outlined both ways to further improve the approximation of the national legislation of the EU member States in the field of copyright and industrial property in the EU, and the prospects for the introduction of common instruments of legal protection of intellectual property throughout the integration. These documents are known more under the name "Green books", which were adopted in 1980-90. The XX century led to the development and adoption by the EU institutions of a number of directives and regulations in the field of intellectual property law.

There are two forms of integration of legal processes in the field of intellectual property within the European Union. In the first form -

harmonization of law - there is a convergence of national legislation of the EU member States in the field of legal protection of intellectual property (which is typical for copyright and related rights). The harmonization of law in the EU is carried out by means of such a legal act as a Directive.

The Directive is binding only on the state (or group of States) to which it is addressed and only on the result to which it is intended. Its distinctive feature is also that the forms and ways of realization of the provisions of the Directive are determined by the state-the destination of the Directive. The Directive should normally be in conformity with an act of national law implementing its provisions. The Directive itself sets a time limit for implementation.

In the second form - the unification of law-there is the introduction of a single instrument of legal protection of intellectual property, operating throughout the EU, not replacing, however, national legal protection instruments. This form is more typical for the sphere of means of individualization of participants of civil turnover and their products (works, services), the right of industrial designs, legal protection of selection achievements in the field of crop production. The unification of law within the EU is carried out through the adoption of regulations. The main features of the regulations-the General application in the member States, the General validity in full and direct (direct) action - determine the significant effectiveness of its provisions. The regulations do not need to be subsequently ratified by member States, implemented into national legislation and cannot be amended by anybody of the member state.

At the moment, intellectual property law in the European Union is evolving more and more by moving away from the principle of “droit d'auteur”, where priority was given, first of all, to the personality of the author, the protection of his personal non-property (moral) rights, to the concept of “copyright”, enshrining the primacy of the economic content of copyright and aimed at “inclusion” of objects of creativity in the fabric of market relations. According to this concept, a work of art is nothing more than an object of market relations (identical to material analogues), and its author is a so - called “creative worker” with all the ensuing consequences.

At the moment, in the choice of areas and areas of unification and harmonization of intellectual property rights in the European Union there is a trend of integration in the field of intellectual property of "new" objects of creative activity and new forms of their use. For example, biotechnological inventions, selection achievements in the field of crop production, computer programs and databases, satellite and cable broadcasting, novelties in the system of copyright powers - the right to rent and transfer to free use objects of creative activity, the use of intellectual property in global information networks, etc. This is due to the fact that the "new" spheres of creative relations and their achievements are to a certain extent easier and better "amenable" to a uniform legal regulation in a number of States that are part of the regional system of cooperation, since in this case there are simply no established traditions of internal regulation of these relations, and therefore the coordination of the will of States in this issue is achievable to a much greater extent.

The specifics of the functioning of market-oriented economic relations within the EU in the field of copyright and related rights in recent years leads to the fact that more and more often the subject of copyright (the author or the subject of creativity) are recognized as legal entities (film, TV and video companies, satellite and cable broadcasting, etc.), and the object composition of the protected results of creative activity is increasingly expanding. This is reflected, in particular, in the field of legal protection of databases, where legal entities can be given a number of powers (the right sui generis) to simple compilation - database, which are not the result of the creative activities of their Creator, and represent only the total effect of financial investment of companies in the search for data, their systematization and representation in the form of a database. Naturally, all this is again determined by the imperatives of the market economy, the need for the primary protection of investment, and not the work of art and its true Creator.

One of the most important vectors of development of intellectual property rights in the European Union is its internationalization. This, in particular, is reflected in the increasing influence of the norms of universal international agreements adopted under the auspices of international organizations on the intellectual property rights of the EU (world intellectual property organization, UNESCO, world trade organization, European patent organization, etc.). One example of this is the accession of the European community on the 30th May, 2005 as a party to the International Convention for the protection of new plant varieties, revised in Geneva on the 19th March, 1991. The said decision was adopted by the EU Council (2005/523/EC) within the framework of the powers provided for in articles 300 and 308 of the EU Treaty.

At the same time, the modern mechanism of legal protection of intellectual property in the EU is more modernized, includes areas of protection that are not sufficiently regulated at the international universal level within WIPO (biotechnological inventions, the right to follow in the field of copyright ("droit de suite"), etc.). As a result, there are problems of lagging behind the mechanisms of the world intellectual property organization from regional (European) systems.

Moreover, there are a number of draft laws that recognize the legitimate use of such methods of consumer restrictions. An example is the North American DMCA (Digital Millennium Copyright Act), a US law enacted in 1998 that contains a package of amendments to the copyright act. It introduces three articles that change the essence of copyright through the adoption of a significant number of non-essential changes. The law stated: "No person shall circumvent a technological measure that effectively controls access to a work protected under this title" (it is forbidden to circumvent technological measures that control access to works protected under this law). In other words, it protects access controls in General, rather than technical protection of exclusive rights, which is becoming less possible due to the development of computer technologies. Similar requirements were subsequently introduced in the WIPO copyright Treaty and in the European Copyright Directive. As a result, the essence of the concept of "intellectual property" is changing, from the unified set of rights established by the state, equal for all parties, to the definition of the individual scope and nature of powers due to the existence of opportunities for coercion of economic or technical nature.

There is another protective organization - Alliance of developers and publishers of commercial software (Business Software Alliance - hereinafter BSA). Members of the Alliance are such well-known companies as Microsoft, Adobe, Macromedia and Symantec. The BSA positions itself as "the voice of the global commercial software industry to governments and the international market" and the purpose of the activity is defined as "promoting a safe and legal digital world". To protect its own interests, the Alliance is focused on interaction with the security forces to a greater extent than with the legislative ones. The small number of BSA members is connected with the specific feature of the market of products of the listed organizations, which are engaged in strict retention of copyright for the published programs, and are focused on the market of "box" edition of programs, which does not provide direct contacts between developers and consumers of products.

Examples of international integrated business structures designed to protect the interests of its members in specific areas, are: Initiative for Software Choice (hereinafter ISC), created to counter the Movement of free software, and in particular, government initiatives for the support (composed of the founder of Microsoft and a few small subsidiaries and affiliated organizations); European information and Communication Technology Association (hereinafter - EICTA), created to fight for the legalization of software patents in Europe.

Such organizations as WIPO (World Intellectual Property Organization), EPO (European Patent Office), and WTO (World Trade Organization) were created to serve multilateral international treaties in the field of intellectual property protection. At the same time, over time, the functions of such organizations are expanding so much that as a result they seek to dictate their own will to the weakest parties to the agreement.

WIPO emerged from the BIRPI legal Bureau, which had existed since 1893, with a staff of seven notaries, whose responsibilities included the storage of texts of international conventions for the protection of exclusive rights (such as the Paris Convention for the protection of industrial property (1883) and the Berne Convention for the protection of literary and artistic works (1886), and the resolution of administrative matters related to them.

WIPO currently employs about 800 people. The annual budget is 410 million Swiss francs (about 315 million USD), which is almost 90% formed by the registration of patents and trademarks, and the rest are contributions of countries-participants of international agreements. In accordance with this activity, the expenditure part of the budget of the organization is formed: the main costs are allocated to "information, training, assistance in the development of laws" mainly, developing and dependent countries; and only a small part - the costs of the administration of the conventions. However, the impact of States parties on WIPO's activities is limited (Mendel P, et al., 2008, 88-99).

The European Patent Office (hereinafter - EPO) was established as the Executive body of the European Patent Convention in 1973, which introduced single "European" patents, mandatory for execution in the European Union. Initially, in order to ensure the principle of equality of all parties to the Convention, it was decided that EPO was not subject to control and full independence (to ensure this, a decision was made on self - sufficiency, funding through patent went). Over time, this has led to EPO lobbying for its own commercial interests, including through an expanded interpretation of patentability under the Convention, without taking into account the interests of the founding countries. Thus, the European patent Convention, as well as the patent laws of most national States, prohibits the issuance of Software patents (patents for algorithms for performing operations or presenting information in computer devices). However, EPO started to issue patents since 1997; only at the beginning of 2000's some representatives of the EU expressed their dissatisfaction with this, which was manifested in the development of the European Directive on software patents only. However, the policy of EPO has not changed. Software patents are terrible because in the conditions of universal computerization their application means the possibility of patenting the majority of economic and organizational operations. The most outstanding public organizations that were able to resist EPO on patenting issues were: Eurolinux (EuroLinux Alliance for a Free Information Infrastructure), EuroRights and FSF-Europe.

5.3. Protection Mechanism in Transferring of Innovations

Achieving strategic competitive advantages in today's global acceleration of scientific and technological progress, reducing the lifetime of new products and processes, as well as the constant increase in the cost of conducting R&D requires not only conducting their own research, but the use of R&D results of other companies, including foreign

International technology transfer (international technology transfer) is a set of economic relations between firms of different countries in the use of foreign scientific and technological achievements.

International documents interpret the concept of "technology" very widely; according to the neoclassical theory, it includes:

- the technology itself (disembodied/dissembled technology), understood as a set of design solutions, methods and processes;
- materialized technology (embodied technology), i.e., technology embodied in machines, equipment, etc.

Accordingly, the subject of the transfer can be both types of objects-both together and separately.

There are several forms of technology transfer in the world market:

- transferring, sale or license of all forms of industrial property (except for trademarks and brand names);
- providing know-how and technological expertise;
- trading of high-tech products;
- provision of technological knowledge necessary for the acquisition, installation and use of machinery and equipment, semi-finished products and materials obtained through procurement, lease, lease or any other means;
- industrial and technical cooperation regarding the technical content of machinery, equipment, semi-finished products, materials;

- consulting and engineering services;
- technology transfer within the framework of scientific and technical production cooperation;
- technology transfer through investment cooperation.

International technology transfer can be carried out at the inter-firm channels of independent foreign firms, and through internal channels of MNC in the case of the introduction in any country office of scientific and technical achievements developed by the organizational unit of the MNC in another country. In modern conditions of increasing expansion of the activities of multinational corporations, a large share of license exchange in the world is carried out through intra-firm trade, which reduces the risk in the conclusion of contracts and guarantees the preservation of scientific and technical secrets.

The process of technology transfer is closely related to the life cycle theory of technology developed By D. Ford and K. Ryan (Nicholas T., 2011, 78-89). They divided the life cycle of the technology into five stages;

1. research and development: technology transfer is not done, as there are only estimates of the potential value of the technology, but the scope and costs of development are unclear;
2. disposal: a new product is produced only in the developing country. The possession of technology is a monopoly, there is no competition. Technology transfer takes the form of exports of goods;
3. technological growth: technology is beginning to be transferred to other developed countries but has not yet been fully developed. As at this stage the volume of technology transfer is gradually increasing, the issue of the cost of the transferred technology becomes relevant;
4. technological maturity: there is a mutual exchange of technological innovations between developed countries, gradually new technology is being improved and standardized, its transfer to developing countries is active. It is becoming widespread, its value

is falling, in a developed country production stops; because of the growing competition from developing countries, the export of goods is replaced by its import, there is a transfer of technology from a developing country to a underdeveloped country;
5. technological decline: investment in technological development is not made, technology transfer is limited to developing countries.

The technology transfer process consists of the following steps:

- identification of need. It includes a study of the economic need for replacement;
- existing technology, market demand requirements, competition factors, comparison of applied and potentially attracted technology (production, availability of resources (human, qualification, material, financial, etc.), availability of related technologies (both in the country and abroad);
- technology evaluation. It is related to the identification of all existing or developing technologies that can meet the need. It includes assessment of availability, acceptability, performance of alternative technologies, and the possibility of their adaptation to country conditions. The trends of technological development and the prospects for the emergence of even more advanced technologies are also considered;
- planning for technology transfer. This includes financial and marketing planning;
- transfer planning - both physical (in the form of transfer of machines, equipment) and in the form of transfer of knowledge, scientific and technical documentation; planning of training;
- planning of material flows; planning the process of technology implementation (search for the most effective way of implementation); planning the processes of management, operation of technology and its modernization;
- implementation of technology transfer. Assessment and selection of the most effective way to implement technology, definition of the

input schedule, organization of personnel training, development of control, management, maintenance and service systems of technology, as well as development of local opportunities to improve technology to meet the needs of the national economy.

Technology is a commodity (though specific), so the most important element in any process of technology transfer is the pricing. Typically, the price of the technology is set in the course of negotiations between the seller and the buyer to conclude a license agreement and takes into account the cost and benefits of the transaction of both parties. Licensing negotiations consist in finding points of agreement in the maximum and minimum prices for the transferred technology offered by both parties.

The economic feasibility of selling technologies is determined by:

1. profit from the development of new technology. Sometimes the sale of technology may be the only opportunity to commercialize scientific and technological achievements due to the lack of necessary production capacity, lack of financial or other resources for self-development of the developed technology, or if the development of scientific and technical results does not meet the objectives and/or development strategy of the company;
2. additional profit from the sale of technology that has already been developed and uses;
3. prevention of illegal use of patented technology by foreign companies;
4. increase in exports due to the implementation of the so-called escort effect: often license agreements are associated with additional supplies of equipment, raw materials, materials. The developer can carry out a paid internship and inspection of the technology buyer's work within a certain period of time;
5. establishing control over the foreign buyer of the technology. It can be achieved by different methods: control of the profits of the buyer through the royalty rate fixed in the license agreement; control over the technical conditions of production; control by conjugate export

of equipment, raw materials and materials; finally, the seller of the technology can establish direct control over a licensee's activities using, for example, as a reward of his actions;

6. conquering new markets. Here, technology transfer is a relatively safe way to test the possibilities of entering the foreign market, and by the time the market is already familiar with the new product, the next step may be the beginning of its production in this market by the developer;
7. elimination of problems related to the export of products produced by this technology (customs, transport, marketing);
8. providing access to another innovation through cross-licensing;
9. the transfer of scientific and technological advances to a technologically strong partner offers greater opportunities for further improvement of the technology with the participation of the purchasing partner.

The economic feasibility of purchasing technology depends on achieving the following goals:

- providing access to the already patented innovation of the highest technical level;
- saving of the cost of conducting own research and development of the technology required. At the same time there is a gain in time; however, almost mandatory adaptation of foreign technology to local conditions reduces the effect of such savings and time;
- lower risk of failure with self-developing necessary technology, to guarantee the practical small-scale mining operations of all technology elements;
- reducing the cost of importing goods produced by this technology. At the same time, local capital and labour are often used more cheaply (particularly in the case of technology transfer to a developing country). However, technology imports can lead to additional costs in the case of large volumes of associated imports;
- possibility to use the good reputation and authority of the licensor;

- use of the trademark, advertising and other marketing advantages of the product;
- providing an opportunity to use the services of licensor's technical specialists if necessary;
- expansion of exports of products carried out with the help of foreign technology;
- providing access to another innovation through cross-licensing;
- the transfer of scientific and technological advances to a technologically strong partner offers greater opportunities for further improvement of the technology with the participation of the purchasing partner (Marcus H., 2012, 77-99).

The economic feasibility of purchasing technology depends on achieving the following goals:

- providing access to the already patented innovation of the highest technical level;
- saving of the cost of conducting own research and development of the technology required. At the same time there is a gain in time; however, almost mandatory adaptation of foreign technology to local conditions reduces the effect of such savings and time;
- lower risk of failure with self-developing necessary technology, to guarantee the practical small-scale mining operations of all technology elements;
- reducing the cost of importing goods produced by this technology. At the same time, local capital and labor are often used more cheaply (particularly in the case of technology transfer to a developing country). However, technology imports can lead to additional costs in the case of large volumes of associated imports;
- possibility to use the good reputation and authority of the licensor;
- use of the trademark, advertising and other marketing advantages of the product;

- providing an opportunity to use the services of licensor's technical specialists if necessary;
- expansion of exports of products carried out with the help of foreign technology.

Due to the multidirectional trends in technological development, the technological policy of many international companies is changing significantly. Multidirectional is determined by regional economic integration and unification in consumer preferences on the one hand, and strengthening the protection of territorial customs, cultures in consumer behavior with the other.

In this regard, there are two possible behaviors in technology transfer:

- result of a one-time acquisition of technology owned by another company;
- within the framework of scientific and technical cooperation of several firms.

International scientific and technical cooperation is a form of relations that involves the interaction of firms of two or more countries in the conduct of scientific and technical activities.

The most promising form of international scientific and technical cooperation today is the creation of strategic alliances between firms from different countries to jointly solve scientific and technical problems. Within the framework of strategic alliances the following interaction between firms is provided;

- joint R&D;
- mutual exchange of scientific achievements;
- mutual exchange of production experience;
- training of qualified personnel.

In the last two decades, the trend of strategic alliances has increased dramatically, especially through alliances of companies in high-tech industries such as pharmaceuticals, telecommunications, civil aviation, semiconductor manufacturing, etc.

The motives that push companies to create strategic alliances are the following circumstances:

- rapid technological development and reduction of the life cycle of goods and processes, and thus reduced R&D time;
- the increasing cost of research in high-tech industries and, consequently, the distribution of costs between firms for joint R&D;
- access to scientific and technological achievements of the alliance partner;
- allocation of risk of failure in joint R&D.

Questions for discussion (Chapter 5):

1. What are the meanings of "technology management" and R&D?
2. How do intellectual property rules help technology's development?
3. What types of R&D do exist in global environment?
4. Why it is important to protect and control the technology?
5. What is the role of alliance and other structures in R&D?

Chapter 6

INNOVATIVE DEVELOPMENT OF TECHNOLOGY ENTREPRENEURSHIP IN INTERNATIONAL BUSINESS

6.1. GLOBAL LEADERSHIP THROUGH INNOVATIONS

Modern large companies operating in global markets are striving to create long-term competitive strategies for organizational leadership. Managers use different approaches for this:

1. Create sustainable competitive advantages,
2. Manage the centers of key competencies,
3. Create mutually beneficial international cooperation,
4. Ensure the safe transfer of knowledge, innovations and technologies.

Adapting to the changing environment requires the highest governing body of the flexible organization, which is reflected in the changes related primarily to technologies, and often the structure and goals of the organization. However, the organization should be sensitive to the appearance of internal stresses, which are not related to the external environment influences. Thus, the emergence of the new organization of professionals with advanced skills and knowledge can lead to a change in production processes or revision control system; purchase of new equipment generally entails a change in the entire process chain and the social structure of the organization.

Obviously, the only organization that can quickly capture and use modern knowledge and technology, use cultural innovations, introduce new forms of work with the staff and constantly improve the ways of working with information, is able to maintain and develop relationships with the institutional environment, to count competitors, support partnerships and meet the public demand.

Successfully implement and disseminate innovations also enable the organization to solve the problem of social structures integration and successfully achieve their goals. In other words, the fulfillment of all the survival conditions of the organization is necessary due to its capacity for constant change; only the changing, dynamic and flexible organization can successfully exist in a complex of political, economic, social and cultural environment. Implementation of intentional and purposeful change should not be in conflict with traditional forms of behavior that have developed in the organization. On the contrary, properly planned and carried out the tradition of innovation able to fill new content, to make the organization more attractive to employees, customers, consumers and the public (Figure 7).

There is no organization that could safely and easily carry changes made in its subsystems. When an organization on the rise, the questions from its workers arise, employees are looking for new forms of activity. Employees will not work if the result is unknown, or if there are elements of risk. Most of the workers through the organization carry out their personal goals and are simply unable to see the perspective of its development; the various groups in an organization have a different perception of innovation.

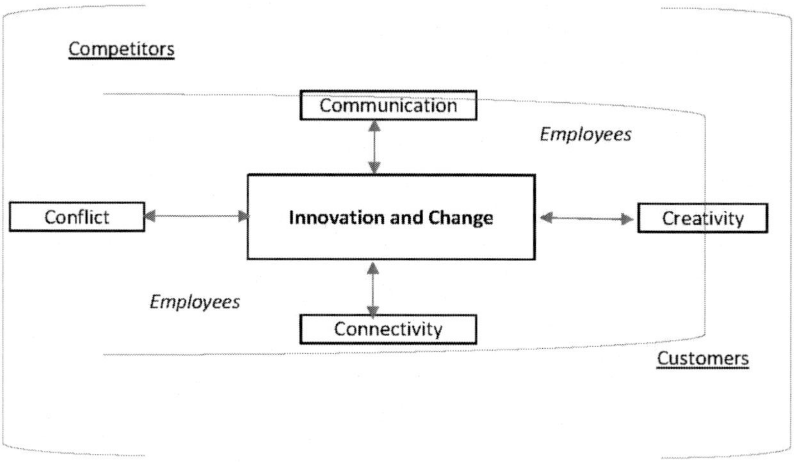

Source: Frankel E.G. Management of Technological Change, Dordrecht Edition, 1990.

Figure 7. C's Global Leadership Model: supporting innovation and change.

It is the most difficult to accept innovations by the middle management, but this is the guarantor of the stability of the organization. Significantly less resistance to innovation have ordinary performers, especially in those organizations where managers have complete trust in the senior management of the organization as the authoritative. However, under the influence of middle management, which is in direct business and personal contact with the artists, the latter may have confidence to innovate and to resist their implementation.

The innovation is the essence of business, for example Peter Drucker says: "business has only two basic functions: marketing and innovation", therefore practically all companies lead innovative activity.

Consulting company PricewaterhouseCoopers (PwC) in a recent survey of managers in large companies (2015-2016) has got the auditing results: only 3% of the top-managers reported, that innovation is not are a priority for the company in the markets, where it works (Lotti F., 2017, 88-90). However, not everyone has the opportunity to innovate activities in a systematic and orderly manner: often it is spontaneously from the enthusiasm of a particular leader/employee, and the innovation strategy absent.

And even significant temporary and financial resources spent to create innovations, do not guarantee the result. To build a trouble-free system reproduction of innovations is a complex and an ambitious task.

For example, most of global companies try to spend more R&D expenses to support innovative activities (Figure 8). Through innovative activity corporations build their competitive advantages.

2013 Worldwide Semiconductor R&D Spending Leaders (Companies with ≥$1 Billion in Spending)

2013 Rank	2012 Rank	Company	Region/ Country	Type	2012 Sales ($M)	2012 R&D ($M)	R&D/ Sales	2013 Sales ($M)	2013 R&D ($M)	R&D/ Sales	13/12 R&D
1	1	Intel	Americas	IDM	49,114	10,148	21%	48,321	10,611	22%	5%
2	3	Qualcomm	Americas	Fabless	13,177	2,655	20%	17,211	3,395	20%	28%
3	2	Samsung	South Korea	IDM	32,251	2,765	9%	34,378	2,820	8%	2%
4	5	Broadcom	Americas	Fabless	7,793	2,318	30%	8,219	2,486	30%	7%
5	4	ST	Europe	IDM	8,364	2,413	29%	8,044	1,816	23%	-25%
7	9	TSMC	Taiwan	Foundry	16,951	1,370	8%	19,850	1,623	8%	18%
6	8	Toshiba	Japan	IDM	11,217	1,710	15%	11,958	1,560	13%	-9%
8	7	TI	Americas	IDM	12,081	1,877	16%	11,475	1,522	13%	-19%
9	13	Micron	Americas	IDM	8,002	909	11%	14,433	1,487	10%	64%
10	6	Renesas	Japan	IDM	9,314	1,901	20%	7,975	1,343	17%	-29%
—	—	**Top 10 Total**	—		168,264	28,066	16.7%	181,864	28,663	15.8%	2%

Source: Company reports, IC Insights

Source: Pivovarov S.E. et al. International management - SPb, Piter Edition, 2015.

Figure 8. Leading R&D global companies.

A new approach to manage global competitiveness is open innovation's creation. There are different approaches how to manage open innovation in global environment:

1. Incubator.

This is a platform for consulting, mentoring and property support innovative companies (start-ups) on the seed stage. The goal is the withdrawal of the company or product on the market, bringing the prototype product to industrial design.

The terms “incubator” and “accelerator” are often are used interchangeably for the designation of the organization providing help entrepreneurs or teams startups at a very early stage. The incubation process is longer, and the accelerator (“accelerator”) gives young innovative companies momentum of development.

There are various models of incubators/accelerators, and directed not only at interaction with external entrepreneurs: sometimes team of the company's employees fits into the incubator to create new products and business models that are not suitable for development within existing business units.

2. *Hackathon.*

For the first time Hackathon passed in 1999. This is a developer forum - “Hackers”, during which experts on software (programmers, designers, managers) in a comfortable environment for them together or breaking into teams decide what task/problem. Such a “brainstorm” tool usually lasts from one day to a week and can lead to the creation of original solutions and products.

Hackathons are held not only for external developers. Many innovative corporations (Facebook, Amazon, Google, Microsoft, and Hewlett Packard) conduct internal Hackathon for their engineers and developers. For example, Facebook like button is known to all and was invented on the inside Hackathon.

3. *Open innovation platforms.*

Platforms for open innovation are Web portals where corporations can formulate its problem for the general public. Such platforms are effective way for small organizations to participate in the decision big problems. This relatively new tool crowdsourcing corporation is active is used as one of the channels open innovation. For example, Russian corporation “Rusal” announces contests on the Innocentive platform; LEGO, IBM, American Airlines announce contests on the platform Chaordix; and the BrightIdea platform is a success from GE, Bosch, Cathay Pacific and Merck.

4. Corporate venture capital.

For a large company, one of the most effective tools for innovative policy is a corporate venture fund. The purpose of its creation is to open a new channel access to innovation and, accordingly, promote scientific and technical development of the company through investment in prospective projects (as a rule, on stage start up and early growth).

The feature of the corporate venture capital is that the corporation operates in the process of venture investment independently (for the most part), not involving for the organization of the transaction professional investment mediator "from the side".

Corporate Venture Financing has become a systemic activity. On its scale, one can judge from this digit: only for the first half of 2016.

GV (Google Ventures) - the current the leader of the corporate venture market invested in more than 30 companies. In such a large-scale the hunting for innovation is fully justified with own venture financial units.

The units that are also working in the same cooperation with corporate services R&D. Corporate Venture Fund can be formed as an internal a division of the corporation (Cisco, Microsoft, StatOil) or a separate external (subsidiary) structure (Intel Capital, Qualcomm Ventures).

Unlike classical venture funds whose task is to provide high return on invested capital, criteria for the success of corporate venture capital capitalists are different. Both in Europe and in the USA primary motives for investing corporate venture funds are strategic rather than financial.

Of course, it is advisable not to lose money, but also to raise high profitability. Synergy and "correctness" are important investments for business development corporations.

According to Global Corporate Venture, there are approximately 1,200 corporate venture units and divisions now in the world. And if in the 1990's and 2000's venture capital divisions/subsidiaries were created mainly in sectors information technologies (Intel, IBM, Samsung, Qualcomm, Comcast, Dell, Google, etc.) and pharmaceuticals, today the branch boundaries are not observed, for example, we can find examples of venture capital in trading, financial, oil and gas, machine-building corporations; all of them also become venture capitalists. This happens because all sectors of the economy are changing and influencing on subversive innovations.

For example, BMW creates a venture fund "BMW" I Ventures in response to the rapid development of electric transport, technologies of autonomous driving and ever stronger penetration information technologies in the processes not only production but also operation Vehicle.

Approximately 20% of global transactions refer to corporate venture capital account for venture industry.

Corporate and traditional (Institutional) Venture capitalists well complement each other and often invest together. The first provide the best industry expertise and access to the client base, the second is better versed in construction companies and the achievement of financial indicators.

Modern global companies try to implement effective model of innovation management, so there are 4 generations of innovation management (Table 11).

Table 11. Four generations of innovation management

Stage	Approach
1	Corporate R&D laboratory
2	Adapted project management methods to R&D
3	Internal collaboration between different functions in the firm
4	Routines designed to make more flexible the conduct of the R&D function through the incorporation of the knowledge of users and competitors

Source: Authors' survey.

Thus, the modern global companies are developing and operating in a complex and contradictory environment. With rare exceptions, the organization must constantly respond to the impact of the external environment by adapting its objectives, structure, technology and policies to changes in external conditions. In this respect, any modern organization should be geared to change; leaders need to understand that change cannot be carried out through orders. This means that managers need to plan and implement innovative process.

Implementation of innovation is closely linked with the process of obtaining and using knowledge, generating ideas and transferring innovations. The process includes information and product implementation, allocation of resources, make decisions emerging ideas and hypotheses, as well as models and schemes, borrowed from the side (Figure 9). The new knowledge can be obtained only when there is a basis of the previous one.

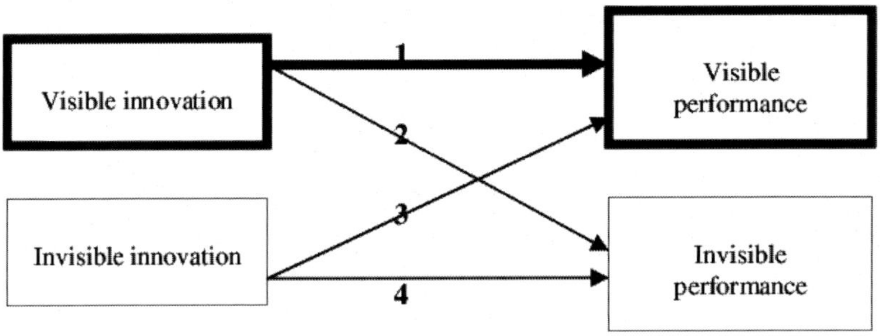

Source: author's survey.

Figure 9. Four essential enables to close the innovation gap.

The specific direction - knowledge management - appeared and started to develop in the scheme of management in the global companies. It includes monitoring of general knowledge, their production system, stored in a proper manner and the efficient and productive use. A serious problem is the classification of inventory, codification, storage of information and the electoral procedure to access it. Some employees have unique knowledge and fear that providing information to others can affect their status as professional skills. Such opportunities are often fully conscious limited while access to information could increase the possibility of its use and application, and provide the basis for new knowledge.

A key requirement for innovation is coming up with new ideas. In the nineties, the emphasis was on creative genius. By applying specific techniques, creativity could be improved. Many new techniques have become available for stimulating new ideas that are relevant and new. At the turn of the 20th century, over 400 definitions of creativity were existed.The concept of simplicity was introduced to simplify some of the complex challenges being posed to the creativity experts; and creative input from other stakeholders became accepted practice for co-creation of value.

Another key requirement for innovation is implementation or uptake of ideas, both commercially and non-commercially. Early involvement of employees and other stakeholders, such as customers, lead users, research units and open innovation agents became accepted practice. Leaders could engage people in new ways to bridge the gaps between people and possibilities. Imitation as a form of innovation has also been acknowledged and some have benefitted from following this approach by copying leading innovations rather than pioneering their own which often allowed them to innovate faster, cheaper and at lower risk for themselves and their recipients.

Based on the insights conveyed, it should be clear that the concept of innovation leadership is still relatively new, yet acknowledged for its importance. Scholarly contributions to the knowledge base have been few and fragmented and lack integration, which serves as further support for what the current study aimed to contribute, namely a competency profile for innovation leaders.

6.2. Core Competence-Based Approach in Global Environment

Many authors consider that competence-based approach can be discussed as 1) the set of individual characteristics of the employee which are directly connected with execution of functional obligations, and 2) more universal personality characteristics and behavioral models (Hamel G., et al., 2005, 145-167). The logical competency structure allows considering knowledge and experience of the employee in various sections of professional activity. The logical competencies can be seized in the course of acquisition of life experience. In this case the qualification is not just the only necessary thing for the solution what kind of specific production objectives can be implemented on a workplace.

It is possible to select the most significant characteristics of personnel competence in the organization:

- Establishment of close interrelation between competence and professional activity;
- Competence possesses the structure consisting from the interconnected and constantly developing elements: skills, knowledge, abilities, etc.;
- Competence is not congenital and it is purchased and accumulates with experience;
- Competence is the concept connected with professional activity of the person.

We try to investigate all definitions of competencies, estimate core competence' model and analyze the linkage between organizational competencies and competitiveness.

The dependence between a core organizational competency and its key personnel competences is not linear, so, the core competency of the company cannot be determined by the simple amount of employee competences, it depends on their configuration and properties of mutually strengthening (availability of synergy effect).

According to this research we prepare the solution, that employee's competences can provide the synergy nature of core organizational competency only in case of their complementarity. In this case, if company wants to improve its competitive level it should follow some management directions:

1. observe existing competencies;
2. provide compliance;
3. manage core competencies.

Two last management functions of the organization are regulated:

1. by activation of informal confidential interaction, that is implemented extremely seldom owing to “closeness” of informal structure for third-party invasion;
2. by traditional training (programming of this action, assessment of effectiveness, ensuring compliance of tasks. In this case employee’s developments are directed by organizational dynamics).

In industrial companies the task of a complementarity of competences finds strategic importance owing to variability of a contour and structure of project structure. Such organization shall provide training process in the permanent mode.

It is important to introduce the concept of American researchers. They consider a personnel competence as set of six components. These components are:

1. Conceptual aspect - perception and judgment of theoretical bases of professional activity;
2. Tool aspect - ownership of basic labor skills;
3. Integrative aspect - possession of a capability to put the theory into practice in case of the solution of professional problems;
4. Contextual aspect - perception of canons of a corporate culture, in which professional activity is performed;
5. The adaptive aspect - possession of skills of change anticipation in external and internal environment and readiness to react to them;
6. Communicative aspect - possession of oral and written skills of interpersonal communication.

This research determinates that core competency is offered as capabilities to develop the available organizational resources on the basis of the effective personnel training system. Such system can follow to creating competitive advantage.

Modern corporations which are operating in the high-tech markets must be adapted to the current pace of development tools and mechanisms. These tools include:

1. the methodology of forming “core competencies”,
2. the creation of support centers “inorganic competencies” (focused on the new “core competencies” creation),
3. practical arrangements. “Open innovation” is tool that provides speed dialing and the development of new competencies on the basis of close cooperation with the market and getting feedback from it.

The “Open innovation” competency matrix is used to prepare an adequate decision on the competence development. This tool helps to select the form of using approach, name the partition of all subsets of the innovation competence unit and provide not only the organic and inorganic expertise (Table 12).

The international practice shows that such corporate giants like Intel, General Electric, Apple, Motorola, Thales, North Grumman and a number of others, use the acquisition of new competencies within the framework of inorganic innovative projects like the most important competitive factors.

For example, Google's innovative complex is presented as a set of separate research teams involved in the development of new technologies and products. Those competencies appear due to the unique corporate system “20 percent time”.

It means the company's philosophy, according to which the company's employees can spend one day a week for the development of new projects not related to their immediate duties. Thus, 80% of their time programmers must deal with the search engine development and advertising services, and the remaining 20%, they can devote to their own projects. Leaders must also be innovative: it is necessary to spend 70% of the time to the main work, 20% - to other projects related to the main job, 10% - to new trends and products (Gupta N, et al., 2013, 56-76).

Table 12. Comparison of organic and inorganic competencies

Criteria	Organic	Inorganic
Competence	Development of the current “core competencies”	The development and acquisition of new competencies
Source	The source of the company acts itself	Internal competencies are actively involved in the competence of the market
The payback period of brief examination of competence development	Projects with medium-term prospects for the return outlet	Projects with long-term prospects for the return outlet
Criteria for making a decision on the development of tight financial decision	Along with finance	Decisive role is decided by the market prospects in a few years and current technological trends

Source: Author’s survey.

Today, the global innovative company carries out strict control of competence-based projects, because the company's management has recognized the value of these innovations. In such way Gmail and GoogleDocs were developed. These company's expenses in R&D are up to 3.7 billion every year (12.63% of total revenues). Thus, professionals and entire teams develop competence largely on their own, decentralized way.

Global practice shows, that any large company should implement its own support system for “inorganic competencies”; and it can be a possible modification of a set of core competencies over time. The task to find new competencies and identify them as an update key becomes a basis to remain competitive acts and find the ability to grow or to borrow knowledge from the market.

When company manages the competences according to the process of developing an organizational strategy, management should clearly identify which organizational competencies are needed to be implemented into this strategy. Organizational competence is a set of competencies of staff which are combined with the ability of organization to achieve specific results. There are examples of organizational competencies:

- the ability to develop new product with minimal costs to the industry,
- the competence in the field of foreign representative offices and branches,
- the competence in the area of customer needs in the development of new product.

6.3. Customization of Innovations in Global Industrial Markets

Commercialization of developments is aimed at obtaining a commercial result and begins with the discovery of the prospects for commercial use of the new development, and ends with the implementation of the development (technology, obtained with its help of the product or service provided) in the market and obtaining a commercial effect (Figure 10).

The process of commercialization of scientific and technical developments, as well as physical, biological and any other processes in nature, society and science, has various parameters at the input (it starts with an idea, a model, a small series) and is multicomponent (includes a different number of stages, different partners, various resources, etc.).

Accordingly, the results at the output (the result of commercialization may be the sale of a license, the conclusion of a contract for further work, co-production, etc.) will be also different.

Scientific activity is a specific branch of the global economy, developing according to its international and domestic laws. The nature of scientific research in various branches of science and technology dictates its own characteristics, its stages of work. Each stage of research and development work is completed by obtaining a specific result that has a certain commercial value.

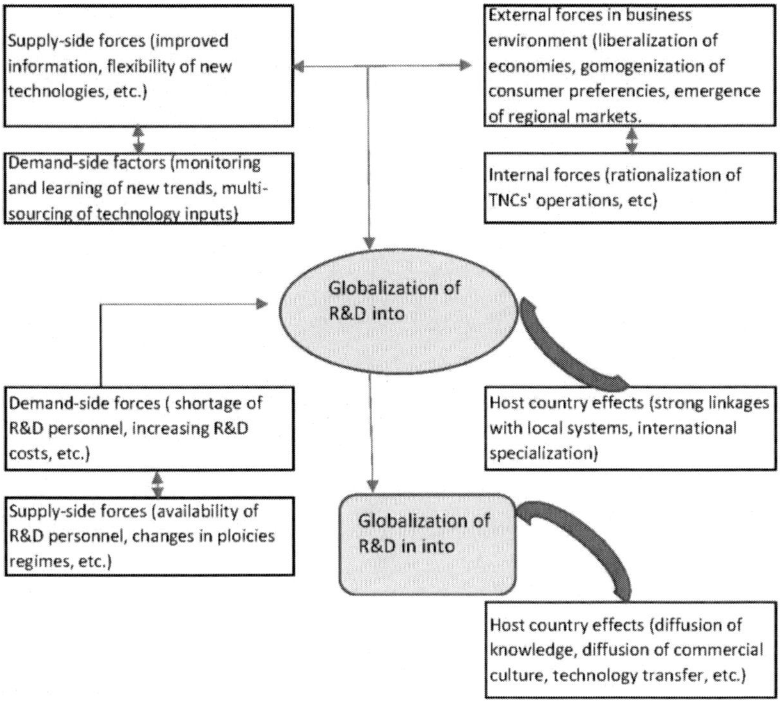

Source: Author's survey.

Figure 10. Globalization of innovations.

However, these results can have a variety of forms. These can be reports on scientific discoveries, experimental and experimental samples of new instruments and installations, new technological processes, as well as new products of high degree of readiness and much more.

Accordingly, the commercialization of these results can take various forms and features, depending on the particular stage of research and development. The results of research and development work in the market should meet all the requirements for the product as an element of the market mechanism, but they have a number of features.

Among the general characteristics for any product, the product in the technology market has significant features, primarily related to the specifics of scientific and technical development as an object of intellectual property. Secondly, the commercial result still lays a long way from scientific and technical development to obtaining its buyer in a specific market. And, at last, the innovation has to bring the novelty to the market.

Among the most important specific characteristics of scientific and technological development as a commodity, we can distinguish the following:

- owner of intellectual property,
- the value of intellectual property,
- state of development (prototype, layout, etc.).

Of particular importance are characteristics common to all types of goods, such as operating conditions, safety and environmental friendliness, competitive advantages and results of comparative tests, engineering services for implementation and operation, and the ability to adapt to the requirements of a particular customer.

It should be noted that the new technology, like any other product, should have a host (owner of intellectual property) and a price (have an estimate of the value of intellectual property).

When solving the problem of entering the world market of technologies, it is necessary to think about the interests and behavior of buyers in this market. The buyer in the industrial market makes a decision based on a detailed review and assessment of available technological alternatives in order to choose the most appropriate option for a particular project or investment strategy taking into account the socio-economic and environmental conditions.

The choice of a suitable development is directly related to the conditions of its use in specific situations. One of the most important factors in the choice of developments, especially for developing countries, is the possibility of competitive production for the target markets.

Accounting for all of these factors leads to the real commodity in the technology market is not the development itself, but a whole technological package that includes, in addition to the actual development, a number of additional elements.

First of all, they pay attention to the degree of development of the so-called engineering services, involving technical assistance in the introduction of the development and operation of equipment, assistance to industrial firms in reducing their costs for maintenance and repair of new equipment.

An important element of the technology package is the ability to adapt the development to the features of its use by a specific consumer, adaptation to local conditions.

High potential commercialization has specific developments, technologies, as well as technical, organizational and other solutions, especially in case of transfer from one industry and application area to others.

The best examples of innovations' customization belong to American and Japanese companies, so let's discuss their strategies of innovation's transferring.

According to the Japanese strategy, the transfer of patented unique OIP to highly specialized industries is carried out in developed countries, and in developing countries we can see the transfer of standardized OIP to traditional industries.

The transfer of standardized, obsolete OIP occurred mainly in the countries of South-East Asia, which have the least technological gap with Japan, through FDI in the creation of joint ventures. C. McMillan confirms that there was a transfer of OIP, which are at the last stages of the life cycle: "... the capital abroad was invested in industries that are experiencing a decline in Japan itself"; and in the Japanese market development of advanced industries and "... exports of industries on the rise". The main task in this case is the transfer of organizational, managerial experience and knowledge based on the achieved level of scientific and technological development. At the same time, technology transfer through training and transfer of experience promote diffusion and transfer of technologies to the territory of the recipient country (Greenhalgh T, et al., 2004, 34-45).

The presence of a minimum technological gap in the international transfer of technology in the domestic market of the recipient country leads to cooperation of donor companies with local firms, to increase labor productivity, to produce modified, improved products and to gradually increase the quality of human and scientific and technical potentials of the recipient entity. Practice confirms that the labor productivity of companies with foreign capital is several times higher than the efficiency of local producers. They are more active in R&D and achieve higher growth in wages and labor productivity, which is due to the use of foreign technologies. It is noteworthy that in developing and transition countries, labor productivity growth was observed in industries whose companies actively interacted with companies of industries with a foreign share of ownership, which indicates the existence of cooperative ties between them. And as firms that have a foreign share of ownership, TNC's affiliated structures often act.

The most attractive countries in the international transfer of Japanese technology packages are the developing countries of the Asian region, Western and Eastern Europe, and South America.

The rate of growth in foreign exchange earnings from exports of Japanese trademarks for the period from 2005 to 2010 in China was 25%, in Taiwan 15%, Thailand 14%, while in the USA 6%, and in the world volume 9%. Thus, Japan's FDI in 2011 was mainly directed to OECD countries (56% of total FDI).

However, the growth rate of FDI inflows for the period 2004-2011 amounted to 212% for this region, and for Asian countries - 325%. The share of the countries of the Asian region accounted for about 35% of Japanese FDI in 2011. The most attractive markets were Malaysia, China, Singapore, Philippines. In addition to these countries and OECD countries, recipients of Japanese FDI were the countries of South America, including Chile and South Africa (OECD, 2018).

FDI contributes to the formation of affiliated structures and the transfer of technology. Thus, the largest share of Japan's affiliated structures falls on Asian countries that are not part of the OECD - 54%, developing countries in Western and Eastern Europe (2%) and Latin America (5%).

Unfortunately, the data of international statistics do not contain information on the value of intra-company exports and imports of goods, services and OIP. The total volume of imports of affiliated structures of developing Asian countries was 38%, and exports - 49%, developing countries of Western and Eastern Europe - 1.7% and 1.9% respectively. The given statistical data confirm that the subjects of the donor country in the case of implementing the Japanese technology strategy are geographically close to countries with cross-cultural similarities.

The North American technological strategy of international technology transfer is radically different from the Japanese one. The strategy of the United States of America, domestic and foreign authors define as profit-oriented. Its implementation is carried out by creating affiliated structures and independent companies in the territory of the host country to obtain full control over its assets, including intangible ones, located abroad with the application of an individual and absorbing market strategy. And the transfer of technology can be carried out in countries where there is a large technological gap. According to foreign scientists, if the technological gap between the North American donor company and the company of the recipient country exceeds 10 years, there is a transfer of "... already obsolete products and newly developed ones; modern equipment is supplied; technical documentation for new technological processes is transferred; confidential commercial information is disclosed; it is possible to use the marketing network of the technology supplier; the experience of international management is transmitted" (Lerner, J. et al. 2007, 77). The basis of this strategy is the transfer of a new OIP, which is patentable to the host country, which can be patented on the territory of the recipient country to win a monopoly on its use and protect its competitive advantages.

High patent activity of non-residents on the territory of developing countries of Asian, Latin American and African regions can be justified by this circumstance: the Philippines (95.1%), Mexico (93.5%), Singapore (90.8%), Brazil (88.1%), South Africa (87.8%), Chile (80%), and India (78.8%) (Royalties and license fees, 1986-2011). These countries do not belong to the main consumers of North American OIP. However, at the beginning of the XXI century the market of these countries became attractive to the United States during the international transfer of OIP.

The largest growth rate of foreign exchange earnings from the exports of North American OIP for the period from 2005 to 2010 is observed in Brazil (29%), India (25%), Taiwan (25%), China (23%), Argentina (21%), South Africa (13%), and the Republic of Korea (12%). It should be noted that the international transfer of technology by the United States to Asian countries (in particular India, Malaysia, Singapore, Taiwan), Latin American (Brazil) and European (Ireland) region is carried out on the basis of the contract “982”, supplying 98% of all necessary elements within two days after the conclusion of the contract.

At the beginning of the XXI century the most attractive region for the transfer of USA technologies has become developing countries and countries with economies in transition. The growth rate of North American FDI in these countries over the period from 2004 to 2010 amounted to 141%, while for OECD countries only 30%. In turn, developing countries in the Asian region in terms of inflows of FDI to the United States achieved a growth rate of about 279% over the same period.

A promising area for the international transfer of North American technologies is their transfer to the countries of South America, in particular in Chile. In 2010, this country received US $4.5 billion of North American FDI, which corresponds to the level of developed countries, such as Germany ($3.2 billion) and Japan ($6.4 billion). Among the countries of the African region can be identified South Africa, which actively attracts the United States OIP and reached the growth rate of US FDI for the period of 2010-2014 years at 59%.

Thus, the international transfer of technology in developing countries and countries with economies in transition mainly takes place according to the strategy of the parent company, whose affiliated structures are located on their territory. Unlike developed countries, about 58% of affiliated structures of TNCs are based on the territory of these States.

Nowadays the market of high-tech services and contract manufacturing is widely spread in developing countries (Brazil, India, China, Malaysia, Taiwan, and Singapore) and countries with transitional economies (Belarus,

Russia, Ukraine, etc.). In developing and transition economies, about 16 million employees (or 80% of the total) are employed in international contract manufacturing, outsourcing of services, franchising, licensing, management contracts, in some countries they provide about 15% of GDP. Developing countries account for about 80% of the world's exports from these activities. In 2011, among the top ten global outsourcing companies in the Global Services 100 ranking, only two were from the US, the rest from Asia (India, China, and the Philippines) and countries with transitional economies (Russia). For example, Belarusian companies such as EPAM Systems, IBA Group, iTransition and Intetics are also included in the list of Global Services 100.

Thus, the strategy of international technology transfer and developing countries with transitional economies can be defined as aimed at the development of contractual relationships not related to equity participation, mainly represented by transactions on cross-border contract manufacturing and service outsourcing. The strategy of the countries is realized by transfer of technologies to the states with cross-cultural similarities and differences due to the implementation of offensive and individual competitive strategies using the principles of market pricing in order to include companies of countries in the global value chains of foreign organizations.

Questions for discussion (Chapter 6):

1. What is the role of core competencies in R&D?
2. Which approaches help managers to create global leadership?
3. What types of global leadership and competitiveness do exist in global environment?
4. Why it is important to create core competencies in technology management?
5. What kind of customization strategies do you know?

Appendices

Appendix A

Case 1

Drawbacks to South Korea's Chosen Innovation Path

South Korea's chosen route to industrial catch-up has its drawbacks. The legacy of siphoning off capital, top talent, and other resources toward developing South Korea's industrial chaebol has come at the cost of a widening gap between big and small firms, and between manufacturing and services. It has created a sharp dichotomy in the industry, a world with "a few big fish and lots of minnows." Outside the chaebol, much of Korean industry is imitative and faces low profit margins and competition from China and other foreign competitors.

SMEs which supply parts and components to the chaebol are disenfranchised compared to their counterparts in Japan and Taiwan (which operate in a similar structure) in that they are locked into fairly closed production networks with very limited decision-making power, which has denied them learning opportunities with diverse firms, both foreign and domestic, to improve internal competitiveness.

Table A-1. Most Problematic Factors for Doing Business in South Korea, 2012-2013

Factor	Percentage of Responses
Policy instability	18.3
Inefficient government bureaucracy	13.4
Access to financing	12.8
Insufficient capacity to innovate	10.3
Restrictive labor regulations	9.3
Tax regulations	6.2
Poor work ethic in national labor force	5.8
Tax rates	5.2
Inflation	5.1
Corruption	4.5
Inadequately educated workforce	3.2
Inadequate supply of infrastructure	2.8
Foreign currency regulations	1.5
Government instability/coups	1.5
Crime and theft	0.2
Poor public health	0.0

Source: From a set list of factors, respondents were asked to select the five most problematic for doing business in their country and to rank them between 1 (most problematic) (WEF 2012).

Question: You are the small company from USA. Try to define strategy entering Korean high-tech market.

Source: Gupta N, Healey D. (2013) Innovation policies of South Korea/Institute of Defense Analyses, Virginia.

Recently, the government has been pushing for financial incentives and technology commercialization opportunities for small and medium-sized firms (although the human capital equation is difficult to address, as employment by chaebol is far more socially prestigious), and their effectiveness remains to be seen. South Korea's service sector is the second smallest in the OECD area, accounting for almost 58% of its GDP (OECD 2012). Only 4 of its 30 largest enterprises are in services; small and medium-sized companies dominate the service sector, accounting for about 80% of output and 90% of employment. Productivity in services is 53% of the productivity level of the manufacturing sector, much below the OECD average of 87%; this mirrors the ratio of wages between the two sectors (OECD 2012) [56].

South Korea also faces other challenges that make it hard to build an entrepreneurial bottom up economy to complement its successful top down state-created companies that dominate the economy. The most problematic factor is policy instability followed by inefficient government bureaucracy. Challenges for small and medium-sized companies are lack of access to financing, insufficient capacity to innovate, and restrictive labor regulations. These challenges and others are ranked in Table A-1.

APPENDIX B

Case 2

Government Leveraging of South Korea's Endowments

The South Korean government has developed a robust science and technology capacity following two parallel tracks:

- *Creation of a state-led research and educational capacity,*
- *Corporate research and development efforts by the country's large conglomerates.*

The government's science and technology policy is implemented in the form of Science and Technology Basic Plans every 5 years. The most recent, the 577 Initiative focuses on sector-specific strategies, including automobiles, shipbuilding, semiconductors, steel, machinery, textiles, and materials. South Korea is also developing in the three broad areas of green technologies, value-added services, and technology convergence, such as the convergence of telecommunications and network technologies into a single system or device (MKE 2010) [46].

South Korea has focused historically on manufacturing but has shifted the focus to services and creation of a knowledge economy as the nation has developed. To achieve the goal of increasing R&D investments as a share of gross domestic product (GDP), the government launched a variety of financial incentives to encourage private investment in R&D, notably by encouraging private financial institutions to turn their collateral-based loans into technological value-based loans. The government also spends extensively on infrastructure; Korea is ranked thirteenth in the world in infrastructure, and leads in broadband penetration (WEF 2012).

The government's investments have been largely effective in spurring S&T-based innovation and progress. South Korean companies have achieved high levels of global competitiveness in leading edge technologies, ranking second globally (behind the United States) in innovation in 2013 (Bloomberg Rankings 2013) [45].

Over the past two decades, South Korea has transformed itself into a leading innovator by adopting Western business practices and making aggressive R&D investments while capitalizing on the strengths of a consolidated manufacturing supply chain.

Today, innovation in the South Korean economy is primarily driven by the private sector, which is dominated by chaebol, such as Samsung, Hyundai, Pohang Iron and Steel Company (POSCO), and LG electronics. These firms typically span a broad spectrum of related and unrelated businesses and control about 70% of South Korea's total spending on R&D (with government contributing about 25%). For example, Samsung is diversified across the food, infrastructure, shipbuilding, life insurance, surveillance, recreation, advertising, and financial industries, among others, leading many to refer to South Korea as the "Republic of Samsung."

South Korean companies have moved from safe technology investments and incremental innovation toward cutting-edge science-based innovation. Capitalizing on future possibilities in science and technology requires disruption and risk taking. Koreans prize efficiency; their desire for success leads them to be highly strategic in their approach. They emphasize planning for R&D in government and industry and using metrics to track success. The government's long-term (technology agnostic) investments in basic science R&D, raised standards for universities, and emphasis on global collaborations will secure Korea's evolution of a knowledge-based economy, but only if paired with an increasing tolerance for risk taking.

Question: Define the main features of Korean innovative economy.

Source: Gupta N, Healey D. (2013) Innovation policies of South Korea/Institute of Defense Analyses, Virginia.

References

Aarons G, Hurlburt M, Horwitz S. (2011) Advancing a conceptual model of evidence-based practice implementation in public service sectors. *Administration and Policy in Mental Health and Mental Health Services Research;* 38(1), pp. 4-23. doi: 10.1007/s10488-010-0327-7.

Aarons G, Wells R, Zagursky K, Fettes D, Palinkas L. (2009) Implementing evidence-based practice in community mental health agencies: A multiple stakeholder analysis. *American Journal of Public Health.* 2009; 99(11), pp. 2087-2095. doi: 10.2105/ajph.2009.161711.

Backer T, Liberman R, Kuehnel T. (1986) Dissemination and adoption of innovative psychosocial interventions. *Journal of Consulting and Clinical Psychology;* 54(1), pp. 111-118.

Beaatriz V. (2017) Mendes Clustering in emerging equity markets//*Emerging Markets Review,* № 8, pp. 194-205.

Berta W, Teare G, Gilbart E, Ginsburg L, Lemieux-Charles L, Davis D, et al. (2005) The contingencies of organizational learning in long-term care: Factors that affect innovation adoption. *Health Care Management Review;* 30(4), pp. 282-292.

Cantwell J, Iammarino S. (2013) *Multinational corporations and European regional systems of innovation.* - London: Routledge, UK.

Cohen W, Levinthal D. (1990) Absorptive capacity: A new perspective on learning and innovation. *Administrative Science Quarterly;* 35(1), pp. 128-152.

Damanpour F, Schneider M. (2006) Phases of the adoption of innovation in organizations: Effects of environment, organization and top managers. *British Journal of Management;* 17(3), pp. 215-236. doi: 10.1111/j.1467-8551.2006.00498x.

Damanpour F, Schneider M. (2009) Characteristics of innovation and innovation adoption in public organizations: Assessing the role of managers. *Journal of Public Administration Research and Theory;* 19(3), pp. 495-522. doi: 10.1093/jopart/mun021.

De Kalbermatten M. (2013) *Corporate Venture Capital in Europe: Objectives, Characteristics and Performance.* Saarbrücken, Germany: AV Akademikerverlag.

Edward de Bono. (2010) *Lateral thinking: a textbook for creativity/* Penguin Adult.

European Innovation Scoreboard 2008/*Comparative analysis of innovation performance/*(2015) Luxembourg: office for official publications of the European Communities, p. 58.

Feldstein A, Glasgow R. (2011) A practical, robust implementation and sustainability model (PRISM) for integrating research findings into practice. *Joint Commission Journal on Quality and Patient Safety.* 2008; 34(4):228-243.

Figueiredo P. (2009) *Technologial learning and competitive performance.* - Cheltenham: Elgar, UK.

Fixsen D, Naoom S, Blase K, Friedman R, Wallace F. (2005) *Implementation research: A synthesis of the literature.* Tampa: University of South Florida, Louis de la Parte Florida Mental Health Institute, The National Implementation Research Network.

Frambach R, Schillewaert N. (2002) Organizational innovation adoption: A multi-level framework of determinants and opportunities for future research. *Journal of Business Research;* 55(2), pp. 163-176.

Freemen Chr., Louca Fr. (2001) *As time goes by: From the industrial revolution to the information*//Oxford University press, Oxford; N.Y., XV, p. 407.

Gallivan M. (2001) Organizational adoption and assimilation of complex technological innovations: Development and application of a new framework. *DATA BASE for Advances in Information Systems;* 32(3), pp. 51-85. doi: 10.1145/506724.506729.

Garland A, Bickman L, Chorpita B. (2010) Change what? Identifying quality improvement targets by investigating usual mental health care. *Administration and Policy in Mental Health and Mental Health Services Research;* 37(1), pp. 15-26. doi: 10.1007/s10488-010-0279-y.

Glasgow R. (2003) Translating Research to Practice. *Diabetes Care;* 26(8), pp. 2451-2456. doi: 10.2337/diacare.26.8.2451.

Glasgow R, Lichtenstein E, Marcus A. (2003) Why don't we see more translation of health promotion research to practice? Rethinking the efficacy-to-effectiveness transition. *American Journal of Public Health;* 93(8), pp. 1261-1267.

Global Innovation Index report. URl//http://www.gii.com (last access 12.12.2018).

Godin G, Belanger-Gravel A, Eccles M, Grimshaw J. (2008) Healthcare professionals' intentions and behaviors: A systematic review of studies based on social cognitive theories. *Implementation Science;* 3(1), pp. 36-48. doi: 10.1186/1748-5908-3-36.

Graham I., Logan J. (2004) Innovations in knowledge transfer and continuity of care. *The Canadian Journal of Nursing Research;* 36 (2), pp. 89-103.

Greenhalgh T, Robert G, Macfarlane F, Bate P, Kyriakidou O. (2004) Diffusion of innovations in service organizations: Systematic review and recommendations. *Milbank Quarterly;* 82(4), pp. 581-629.

Gupta N, Healey D. (2013) *Innovation policies of South Korea*/ Institute of Defense Analyses, Virginia.

Hamel G., Prahalad K., Thomas G., D. (2005) *O'Neill Strategic flexibility*//Peter, pp. 115-118.

Hayati B, BPTT 3133 *Technology Transfer in Business* [Website]. URL: http://www.slideshare.net/nabilahnajah/sem-5-tt-week-1?from_search=1. (last access: 05.04.2019).

Hoffman, K., Parejo, M., Bessant, J., and Perren, L. (1998). Small firms, R&D technology and innovation in the UK: A literature review. *Tec novation,* 18(1), pp. 39- 55.

Horwitz S, Chamberlain P, Landsverk J, Mullican C. (2010) Improving the Mental Health of Children in Child Welfare Through the Implementation of Evidence-Based Parenting Interventions. *Administration and Policy in Mental Health and Mental Health Services Research;* 37(1-2), pp. 27-39. doi: 10.1007/s10488-010-0274-3.

Jagosh J, Salsberg P, Macaulay A, Bush L. (2011) Realist Review: An Introduction; *Paper presented at the Canadian Public Health Association* (CPHA) Meetings; Montreal, Canada.

Kim J. and Han J. (2014) Differentiated Effects of Product Strategy and CEO Characteristics on Venture Firms` Growth: The Moderating Role of Organizational Life Cycle Stage. *Journal of Technology Innovation,* 22(1), pp. 25-58.

Klein K, Sorra J. (1996) The challenge of innovation implementation. *Academy of Management Review;* 21(4), pp. 1055-1080.

Lakshminarayanan A. *Technology Transfer by Altacit Globa* [Website]. URL: http://www.slideshare.net/altacitglobal/technology-transfer-9641953. (last access: 08.02.2019).

Lerner, J. and Wulf, J. (2007) Innovation and Incentives: Evidence from Corporate, R&D. *Review of Economics and Statistics,* 89(4), pp. 634-644.

Levin R, Klevorick A, Nelson R, and Winter S. (1987) Appropriating the returns from industrial research and development. *Brookings Papers on Economic Activity*, pp. 783-820.

Lotti F., Santarelli E. and Vivarelli M. (2009) Defending Gibrat's law as a long- run regularity. *Small Business Economics,* 32, pp. 31- 44.

Lowe R. (2001) *The role and experience of start-ups in commercializing University invention.* In G. Libecap (Ed.) Entrepreneurial inputs and output. Amsterdam: JAI Press.

Main Science & Technology Indicators (MSTI) [Websiate]. URL: www.oecd.org/dataoecd/18/38/41559779.pdf (last access: 02.03.2019).

Mansfield E. (1986) Patents and innovation: an empirical Study. *Management Science,* 32, 2, pp. 173-181.

Marcus H. (2012) Patent management in entrepreneurial SMEs: a literature review and an empirical study of innovation appropriation, patent propensity, and motive. *R&D Management,* 43(1), pp. 21-36.

Mendel P, Meredith L, Schoenbaum M, Sherbourne C, Wells K. (2008) Interventions in organizational and community context: A framework for building evidence on dissemination and implementation in health services research. Administration and *Policy in Mental Health and Mental Health Services Research;* 35(1), pp. 21-37. doi: 10.1007/s10488-007-0144-9.

Meyer A, Goes J. (1988) Organizational assimilation of innovations: A multilevel contextual analysis. *Academy of Management Journal;* 31(4), pp. 897-923.

Mitchell S, Fisher C, Hastings C, Silverman L, Wallen G. (2010) A thematic analysis of theoretical models for translational science in nursing: Mapping the field. *Nursing Outlook;* 58(6), pp. 287-300. doi: 10.1016/j.outlook.2010.07.001.

Nicholas T. (2011) Did R&D firms used to patent? Evidence from the first innovation surveys. *The Journal of Economic History,* 71(4), pp. 1029-1056.

OECD, *"Reviews of Innovation Policy: Korea",* 2018, http://www.oecd.org/sti/inno/oecdreviewsofinnovationpolicykorea.htm.

OECD, *"Economic Surveys: KOREA",* 2018 http://www.oecd.org/eco/surveys/Overview_Korea_2014.pdf.

Oldenburg B, Glanz K. (2008) Diffusion of innovations. In: Glanz K, Rimer BK, Viswanath K, editors. *Health behavior and health education,* San Francisco: Jossey-Bass, pp. 313-333.

Panzano P, Roth D. (2006) The decision to adopt evidence-based and other innovative mental health practices: Risky business? *Psychiatric Services,* 57(8), pp. 1153-1161. doi: 10.1176/appi.ps.57.8.1153.

Pavitt K. (1982) R&D, patenting and innovative activities: a statistical exploration. *Research Policy,* 11(1), pp. 33-51.

Pawson R, Greenhalgh T, Harvey G, Walshe K. (2005) Realist review: A new method of systematic review designed for complex policy interventions. *Journal of Health Services Research and Policy;* 10 (Suppl 1), pp. 21-34. doi: 10.1258/1355819054308530.

Perlitz M. (1997) I*nternationales Management.* Stuttgart: Lucins & Lucins.

Popay J, Roberts H, Sowden A, Petticrew M, Arai L, Rodgers M, et al. (2006) *Guidance on the conduct of narrative synthesis in systematic reviews: A product from the ESRC methods program.* Retrieved from http://www.lancs.ac.uk/shm/research/nssr/research/dissemination/publications.php.

Porter M. (1988) *The competitive advantage of nations.* - 12 Ed. The Free Press.

Porter M. (2003) *Competition. - Publishing House "Williams",* St. Petersburg, p. 423-426.

Propharma Group, Approach to Technology Transfer [Website]. URL: http://www.slideshare.net/ProPharmaGroup/approach-to-technology-transfer-bob-beall-19009502?from_search=3 (last access: 08.02.2019).

Rassenfosse G. (2012) How SMEs exploit their intellectual property assets: evidence from survey data. *Small Business Economics,* 39(2), pp. 437-452.

Roger M. (2004) Networks firm size and innovation. *Small Business Economics,* 22, 16, pp. 141-153.

Roger M. (2003) *Diffusion of innovations.* 5. New York: Free Press.

Royalties and license fees, 1986-2011//U.S. Department of Commerce, Bureau of Economic Analysis [Electronic resource]. - 2011. - Mode of access: http://www.bea.gov/international/international_services.htm 27.10.2012. - (date of access: 27.08.2019).

Sang Ch. (2014) The analysis of strategic management of Samsung Electronics company through Generic Value Chain Model.

International Journal of Software Engineering and Its Applications, Vol. 8, No. 12, pp. 133-142.

Scherer F. (1983) The propensity to patent. *International Journal of Industrial Organization,* 1(1), pp. 107-128.

Schumpete J. (1982) *The Theory of Economic Development.* - Transaction Publishers.

Selin A. (2007) To what South Korea owes Success in Innovation, *Journal of Substance Abuse Treatment;* 41 (3), p. 23-29.

Simpson D. (2002) A conceptual framework for transferring research to practice. *Journal of Substance Abuse Treatment;* 22(4), pp. 171-182.

Solomons N, Spross J. (2011) Evidence-based practice barriers and facilitators from a continuous quality improvement perspective: An integrative review. *Journal of Nursing Management;* 19(1), pp. 109-120. doi: 10.1111/j.1365-2834.2010.01144x.

Sox H. (2010) Comparative effectiveness research: A progress report. *Annals of Internal Medicine;* 153(7), pp. 469-472.

Stetler C. (2001) Updating the Stetler Model of research utilization to facilitate evidence-based practice. N*ursing Outlook;* 49(6), pp. 272-279. doi: 10.1067/mno.2001.120517.

Sul Ch. (2008) *Innovation, competitiveness and growth: Korean Experience.* Seoul, p. 54-65.

Sutton J. (1997) Gibrat's legacy. *Journal of Economic Literature,* 35, pp. 40-59.

Tabak R, Khoong E, Chambers D, Brownson R. (2012) Bridging research and practice: Models for dissemination and implementation research. *American Journal of Preventive Medicine;* 43(3), pp. 337-350. doi: 10.1016/j.amepre.2012.05.024.

Tabak R, Khooong E, Chambers D, Brownson R. (2012) A Narrative Review and Synthesis of Frameworks in Dissemination and Implementation Research; *Paper presented at the 5th Annual NIH Conference on the Science of Dissemination and Implementation:* Research at the Crossroads; Bethesda, MD.

Tan J. (2016) Growth of industry clusters and innovation: Lessons from Beijing Zhongguancun Science Park//*Journal of Business Venturing,* № 21, pp. 827-850.

Tavares A. (2016) *Multinationals, clusters and innovation: does public policy matter.* - Basingstoke: Palagrave Macmillan, UK.

Teece D. (1986) Profiting from technological innovation: implications for integration, collaboration, licensing and public policy. *Research Policy,* 15, 6, pp. 285- 305.

Thumm N. (2004) Motives for patenting biotechnological inventions; an empirical investigation in Switzerland. *International Journal of Technology Policy and management,* 4(3), pp. 275-285.

Urban development: innovation plus the potential of cities [Website]. URL: http://www.tula-forum.ru/researches/inno/part2/ (last access: 15.03.2019).

Valente T. (1996) Social network thresholds in the diffusion of innovations. *Social Networks;* 18(1), pp. 69-89. doi: 10.1016/0378-8733(95)00256-1.

Weinstein N, Sandman P, Blalock S. (2008) The precaution adoption process model. In: Glanz K, Rimer B, Viswanath K, editors. *Health behavior and health education.* 4. San Francisco: Jossey-Bass; pp. 123-147.

Williams C. and Lee S. (2009) Exploring the Internal and External Venturing of Large R&D Intensive Firms. *R&D Management,* 39(3), pp. 231-246.

WIPO Statistics Database: Statistics on Patents [Website]. URL: http://www.wipo.int/ipstats/en/statistics/patents/ (last access: 08.03.2019).

World receipts of royalties and license fees by region, 2009 and 2010 (2011)//World Trade Organization [Electronic resource]. - Mode of access: http://www.wto.org/english/res_e/statis_e/its2011_e/its11_trade_category_e.htm. (date of access: 01.04.2019).

World Development Indicators report (2014), "Foreign Direct 2014" http://datacatalog.worldbank.org/

World Bank report (http://databank.worldbank.org/data/reports/last access 20.12.2018).

Wong G, Greenhalgh T, Pawson R. (2010) Internet-based medical education: A realist review of what works, for whom and in what circumstances. *BMC Medical Education;* 10(1), p. 12.

https://www.msci.com/ (last access 01.12.2018).

http://www.globalcorporateventuring.com/article.php/12794/why-every-company-in-the-fortune-2000-will-have-a-venturecapital-arm. (lasst access 31.01.2019).

About the Author

Olga A. Shvetsova
Assistant Professor,
Korea University of Technology and Education

Assistant Professor at Korea University of Technology and Education (South Korea) since 2016. She graduated Saint-Petersburg State University of Economics (Russia) in 2004. In 2011 she got PhD there.

She actively provides guest lectures in EU and makes research review for some professional societies (IEEE, IBIMA). She published more than 25 research papers and 5 academic books in the fields of international business, innovation management and global HRM.

Annually she develops courses for on-line MBA in EU and participates in international research projects. Olga A. Shvetsova has “Best Teaching” award in 2017 and “Best Young Scientist” in 2015.

INDEX

D

E

F

G

H

I

J

K

L

M

N

O

P

Q

R

S

T

U

V

W

Related Nova Publications

Strategic Rethinking: Connecting Local-Global Business Models

Editors: Rajagopal, PhD and Divya Kirti Gupta

Series: Business Issues, Competition and Entrepreneurship

Book Description: This edited volume spread across fourteen distinguished articles aims at bringing together rich discussions on global-local convergence in reference to emerging markets. The impact on business-to-business and business-to-consumers imperatives, global-local convergence, and vice-versa effects that are driving the national economy are discussed through conceptual and empirical research papers.

Hardcover ISBN: 978-1-53616-835-8
Retail Price: $160

Contributions on Applied Business Research and Simulation Studies

Editors: Orlando Gomes and Mariya Gubareva

Series: Business Issues, Competition and Entrepreneurship

Book Description: This book is a commemorative edition of the 260th anniversary of the Lisbon Accounting and Business School (ISCAL), one of the oldest business schools in Europe. The book collects a series of contributions from teachers and researchers of ISCAL, offering a state-of-the-art picture of the research conducted in this higher education institution.

Hardcover ISBN: 978-1-53616-450-3
Retail Price: $195

To see a complete list of Nova publications, please visit our website at www.novapublishers.com